Women in Wa

Published by Giant Killer Publishing

SmallestSoldier.com

ISBN 979-8-218-57357-7

Printed in the United States of America

WOMEN IN WAR

THE INCREDIBLE ACCOUNTS OF HISTORY'S BRAVEST WOMEN WARRIORS FROM NURSES IN NAM TO OUR FIGHTING COMBAT VETS

DAVID A. YUZUK

"And the truth is that all veterans pay with their lives. Some pay all at once, while others pay over a lifetime…"

- J.M. Storm

Contents

The Vietnam Women's Memorial by sculptor Glenna Goodacre
on the National Mall in Washington, DC.

Introduction

When we think of women in war, the image of Joan of Arc usually comes to mind. Arc led French forces against the English during the Hundred Years' War. Her leadership inspired troops and challenged contemporary notions of female subservience. But Joan of Arc wasn't the exception; history has often overlooked women's service and sacrifice in war.

Women have participated in all capacities during conflicts, challenging traditional gender roles and contributing to military efforts. Women have been instrumental in warfare since antiquity. In ancient cultures, such as those in Egypt and the Celtic tribes, women often took up arms alongside men. Viking women known as shield maidens participated in the front lines of the bloody battles, defying the era's gender norms.

Our women warriors have paved the way for greater participation in the armed forces, reflecting broader changes in societal attitudes toward gender roles. As we continue to recognize and honor their contributions, it becomes clear that the history of warfare is also a history, or her-story, of women—one that deserves to be celebrated and remembered. This book is a journey through time, terrain, and conflicts.

My name is David Yuzuk, and I'm a retired police officer from Aventura, Florida. My journey into researching war heroes started when a tiny homeless man named Richard Flaherty uttered the words, "It's time I tell you who I really am." Ten days later, that man would be killed, and I would spend the next four years investigating his incredible life.

After I published *The Giant Killer,* a book about his life, I needed a way to get the story out to the world. I started with a small Facebook page with only a handful of followers. As I posted stories about my project, an amazing thing started to happen.

More followers, whom I now call members, started coming on board and sharing their stories of war heroes. As the members continued to grow so did my education on these extraordinary soldiers who fought with gallantry and heroics above and beyond anything Hollywood could dream of.

We added more war heroes from different times, military branches, and countries to our page every week. The members loved these stories so much that we started getting requests to make a compilation book. In 2023, I released my first war hero compilation book: *Giant Killers, War Heroes, and Special Forces Legends.*

Two years later, in a world of discourse and internet trolls, I stumbled upon the one subject that all my most hardened internet critics universally agreed upon in a positive light: women who served in the military. My education in this world started with comments from my Vietnam vets when I posted my first few stories about Army nurses in Nam.

The outpouring of respect for their service taught me that these women had shown a level of bravery, professionalism, and patriotism that was underappreciated by us civilians. Only the men who served with these angels in fatigues knew how vital their life-saving roles were to the average infantryman or grunt. That led me on the path to learn more about the history of our Giant Killer women warriors.

The first person I reached out to for help and advice was the woman on the cover of this book, Vietnam Nurse Ginny Dornheggen. Years before, I had written an article about Ginny and her service, and only a month later, I received a message from her.

David,

Recently, a friend Googled my name and found your write-up of my Army Nurse service. He said it was one of the most well-written stories he'd read about my experience!

I then took the time to research it. I want you to know how healing it was to read the comments. Never have I read or even seen people's thoughts of what I did described so thoughtfully. I am not sure how you even found my story, but I thank you for sharing it. It gave me the opportunity to read and know people really do care about what our Vietnam veterans experienced.

—Ginny Deardorff Dornheggen

In my first phone call with Ginny, I instantly knew I had to tell their unique story from their combat boots. Ginny set my feet moving on this path and introduced me to my next incredible Vietnam vet, Army nurse Laura Hines Kern, whose story follows Ginny's.

I tell any of my friends who want to write books that if your heart is in the right place and you're available to listen, you will meet the most extraordinary people you can imagine. This book of women's heroes is a testament to how lucky I've been to interview these incredible warriors.

To be part of our team to help select the next group of Giant Killer heroes, please join our Giant Killer social media pages on Facebook, Instagram, YouTube, TikTok, and several other well-known platforms. Please tell us about the heroes you think we missed and the new ones we may still haven't yet heard of. God bless you all for keeping the memories of these heroes alive.

—David A. Yuzuk

Nurses in Nam

Virginia "Ginny" Lee Dornheggen

I thought I was going to die that day!

★★★

My name is Ginny Dornheggen, and I was a US Army nurse in Vietnam. One of the most terrifying experiences of my life happened on January 6, 1971, when the Viet Cong detonated an allied ammunition depot about a mile from the hospital where I worked. The blast was caused by the detonation of approximately five thousand tons of ammunition.

The thunderous sound came seconds before the shock wave blast hit, blowing out our doors and windows and knocking everything around. It sounded like the loudest sonic boom you can imagine going off right above you. The ongoing secondary explosions lasted into the early hours of the morning.

It was a night shift, as usual—strangely, I seemed to always be on duty whenever we were hit. It was the first time I had experienced enemy activity so close to us. Before that, I sometimes heard and saw firefights going on approximately a mile from the base. You would first hear the AK-47s and machine guns rattling; then you'd see our soldiers' M16 bullet tracers going up and back.

I had been in-country for about a month and a half, and at that point, I was becoming somewhat complacent, thinking that maybe the worst was behind us. The routine of war had settled into a slow rhythm, and I was letting my guard down.

As I walked to work that night, I felt a false sense of security. With ten and a half months in the army still ahead, I convinced myself that things were manageable. But then, at around two o'clock in the morning, the ground shook violently. The loudest explosion I had ever heard erupted, and I feared the mortar had struck the building next to our hospital, where the doctors slept.

Overcome with fear, I ducked under a metal desk in the recovery room, thinking we were being overrun. My body trembled and I prayed fervently. As the power went out to add to the terror, the interior became pitch black. I don't know exactly when the backup power generators kicked in, but they did at some point during the mayhem.

The chaotic noise of shouting nurses in the Intensive Care Unit jolted me back to reality. I realized I couldn't stay hidden, so I grabbed my flak jacket and helmet and hurried the short distance to the ICU. At that point, we had in our care several American soldiers, a handful of civilians, and an enemy prisoner of war [POW].

Our priority was to protect the soldiers first. We lifted them up, placed them on cots, shoved them under beds, and used other mattresses to shield them from flying glass and shrapnel. After tending to the soldiers, we attended to the two civilian women and then the Vietnamese men.

Last in line was a POW who had tripped a landmine and was in a body cast. Usually, it took five people to care for him—two nurses and three corpsmen. Despite the chaos, another nurse and I picked him up, and I managed to get him onto a cot and under a bed, hoping his body cast would offer some protection since we had run out of mattresses.

Before the explosion, our unit had windows with protective tape and wooden doors. Afterward, the windows were shattered, doors blown in, and we were left with emergency power. One of my fellow nurses rested her head on a desk as we prepared for the day shift.

4

We had a patient with a tracheotomy tube who required suctioning, so another nurse and I crawled on our hands and knees, attending to his tubes while managing his oxygen needs.

The experience was an intense lesson in the dangers of complacency in a war zone. We eventually grew accustomed to the distant explosions, but the shock of that night stayed with me to this day. The sheer force of the blast was overwhelming, and it was a sobering reminder of the unpredictable and hazardous nature of war.

My journey into the military started from a quiet life growing up in Gettysburg, Pennsylvania. As kids, we were often asked to participate in the Memorial Day parade, carrying flowers from our gardens to place on the graves of unknown soldiers at the Gettysburg National Cemetery.

As my friends and I walked among the low, semi-circular gray stones, I was struck by the sight of so many unnamed graves marked only by a small American flag where we were to place our flowers. I remember feeling a deep sadness, wondering about the stories behind all those blank stones. Little did I know that this sense of sorrow would resurface years later, intensified by my experiences in Vietnam. Unlike any other conflict in American history, the Vietnam war left a unique and profound domestic trauma to our country.

As the Vietnam War was intensifying on the other side of the world, I started studying to be a nurse. I remember a few times when I'd put my textbook down to listen to the somber news broadcasts about the war crackling through my radio.

During my junior year of college, a conversation with a fellow nursing student sparked a transformative idea: Why not use my medical skills to serve my country in its time of need? This realization of doing my part for my country propelled me into joining the Army student nurse program during my senior year.

My life in the military started with basic training at Fort Sam Houston and then being assigned to Walter Reed Army Medical

Center. By 1970, I was deployed to Vietnam and stationed with the 67th Evacuation Hospital.

The 67th Evac deployed initially to Qui Nhon, Vietnam, in October 1966 and moved to Pleiku in 1972. The 67th participated in fifteen campaigns during the Vietnam War and was decorated with three meritorious unit commendations.

Almost all our patients arrived by helicopter, the Hueys, also known as "choppers" and "Dustoffs." After only a few weeks, I could tell the difference between the distinctive sound the Hueys made with their rotator blades and the blades of the smaller OH-6 Loach scouting helicopters. So I always knew when we were about to get busy.

The medics in the field performed initial emergency care, such as stabilizing airways, starting IVs, and controlling bleeding as much as possible. When a Dustoff was called, it gave the wounded soldiers a glimmer of hope, signaling that help was on the way.

Thanks to the dedicated medics and the Dustoff helicopter crews, we were able to save many young men. If they weren't under fire, the injured could reach the hospitals in less than ten to twenty minutes. In the Vietnam War, there was no clear frontline, so hospitals were considered part of the battlefield. As a combat nurse, my role demanded the highest standards of care in any situation. Critical thinking was essential to navigate the constant challenges and maintain effective care.

The only injured I remember that came in by jeep or bus were civilians injured by mines or vehicle accidents. There was no such thing as an ambulance. If one of the civilians was hurt or something, maybe a military truck, a Duce and a half, brought them in, or maybe on a jeep. Sometimes, the local people would bring them in on wheelbarrows, so to speak.

We worked twelve hours a day, six days a week, and when there were mass casualties, we worked sixteen to eighteen hours daily. When we got off duty, we were so exhausted we just crashed. You slept when you could. Sometimes, you would only sleep four hours, and then you'd go right back to work.

We wore army fatigues all the time. It was not like Saigon Hospitals. In Saigon Hospital, they wore white uniforms. We were in our fatigues and combat boots—big leather boots that had absolutely no cushioning and needed constant polishing.

By the time I got to the 67th Evac, there was a constructed wooden building that had no windows in it. Our hooch was a room that held two people, and then you'd have a bathroom in between two rooms. The word hooch was a slang word that started in the Korean War and basically meant a simple living space or a thatched hut, and in Nam, ours were always surrounded by sandbags.

The base was smaller than they are in Da Nang, but it was undoubtedly well-constructed. It wasn't like the T.V. show 'MASH'—we did not have tents strewn around. We had concrete buildings, and we also had Quonset huts, which looked like chicken coops. There were no windows, but we did actually have air conditioning.

The work was not only challenging physically but also psychologically. We were constantly tested. There was this time several soldiers were ambushed on a mountain pass and required surgery. One was a newly married nineteen-year-old with his right arm blown off at the shoulder. His left arm was amputated above his elbow. Both eyes were bandaged, but he had lost his left eye, and his right eye was questionable.

As he woke up from anesthesia, he became very restless and tried to place his arms down, so he kept lifting his chest up, trying to put it down, and yelling, "Nurse, I can't put my arms down." At this point, it was the wee hours of the morning when all of this was occurring, and the doctor had told me that I was not supposed to say anything to him about his condition.

I sedated him for pain and hoped that it would also help his anxiety, but his anxiety continued, and it increased the agitation. As nurses, we felt that he needed to understand what was going on so we could calm him down.

I explained his injuries in his arms and left eye, and hopefully, that his right eye would be good. His initial response was, "Great, now I'll be selling pencils for the rest of my life." I sat down beside him and placed my hand on his chest, and I told him there would be no time for him to do that because someone as strong-minded as he and determined had better things to do with his life, his mind, and his heart, he was with us a little more than fourteen days.

Every day, one of us nurses would sit down and write a letter to his new wife that he dictated. In turn, when we did get his mail, we read his letters to him. He was finally sent back to the States for further surgeries in rehab.

He wrote back to us to let us know he would be among the first soldiers to receive the newest mechanical arm, which was top-of-the-line. It was these little victories that kept us going. That we were where we needed to be. That we were doing what needed to be done.

He was able to see out of his right eye and especially thanked us for all that we did. That young man taught us all how to be strong, deal with anger and pain, and remain brave during life's most unexpected misfortunes.

We were constantly being pushed to the limits as we ensured we provided the best care we could given the circumstances.

Children were also victims of war. A child I cared for found a phosphorus flare, thinking it was a toy. These were used at night to check for enemy intruders.

This flare, however, was a dud and came apart as he played with it, burning his little body with the white powder. Phosphorus continues to burn even after being cleaned off with water and disrupts the body's electrolyte system. This little guy had a cardiac arrest while I was caring for him, and he didn't make it.

Many of us would take turns going on MedCAP missions, which stood for the Medic Civic Action Programs. There was a leprosarium was near our hospital, and the French nuns ran it.

When the French were in Vietnam, they cared for these poor souls, the banished people with leprosy.

We would perform amputations of the extremities that were affected by this mutilating disease. In appreciation for our service, the nuns would give us a fabulous French cuisine meal and allow us to use their private beach area on the South China Sea, safe and away from all the fighting.

The Punji stick injuries our soldiers endured were really gruesome. The North Vietnamese and the Viet Cong would dig these holes in the jungle floors, and then they would put either excrement or poisons on the tips of these bamboo spears.

They would put these spears inside these holes, then cover them with a brush to conceal them. Our soldiers patrolling in the jungles would fall into those traps. When they fell into these pits, their legs would get scraped, stabbed, or impaled by these medieval Punji sticks.

Time was the critical factor in treating those wounds because of the poisoned tips. If it's half a day or more, that puts them at much more risk than within a few hours. You also have to understand the physical status of these young soldiers. They didn't have the protein or the hydration that they needed.

That's something I don't think a lot of people think about. You're talking about humans who are living on tiny amounts of food, dehydrated from being in the heat and humidity of the jungle, and then getting injured, which changes everything. So their bodies were challenged all the time. Even as young teenagers and men, that was really difficult. That's not even factoring in the mosquitoes, leeches, and other insect bites and rashes causing open wounds on their skin.

There were many ugly things besides just the Punji pits. Due to the poor condition of the water, there were intestinal worms. Sometimes, when you pull a colostomy bag off a patient, the worms are there, and you have to clean the skin and the site. Some of these parasites were quite large and nasty.

The pressure of the job reached a point where I had to ask to be relieved from the ICU and the recovery duties as I was overwhelmed with the stress. My request was approved, and I was given one month in the orthopedic ward that shared a makeshift drug ward. It was where we would place the drug addicts that we could help. At that point, most of them were going through withdrawal, which was highly traumatic for all of us.

It wasn't all doom and gloom, and this story is very close to my heart. We once got a surprise visit from this beautiful woman, Phyllis George, Miss America in 1971, and her entourage. I had already worked ten hours that day when she came through our unit. They were dressed so beautifully in civilian clothes, with makeup and hairdos, and I was in my usual fatigues and combat boots.

One of the soldiers that I was caring for had both arms amputated and could not sit up by himself. As I was helping to hold him up, Phyllis George came over and spoke to him for several minutes.

As I laid him back down, I asked him, "Wouldn't it be great if all of us nurses could look that good?" He gave me the biggest smile and said, "They don't hold a candle to what you mean to us and to what you are." I leaned down, kissed him on his forehead, and told him I would never forget him here. He supported me when I was caring for him. When I turned around, someone had taken a photo of me. (Photo used in the beginning of this chapter)

My Freedom Bird, which took me home, was on November 21, 1971, a year to the day that I was deployed. When I got back to the world, I never thought I had any anxiety issues as I hadn't fought in the field. At least, that's what I felt. However, these feelings had been suppressed and came out by my reaction to a car backfiring. I found myself on the sidewalk.

On the 4th of July, I found myself under the bed after a cherry bomb went off, and my recurring nightmare of being overrun was a reminder of my past few months. However, I still felt okay. In 1982, the Vietnam Veterans Memorial, best known as "The Wall," was created. My first encounter visiting the wall was traumatic.

Looking at the black and white wall, I realized how many did not make it home. For those of you who have not seen it, you cannot imagine how mere stone and engraving can have so much impact.

The names start out so few and low to the ground. As you go deeper, the names go higher until you feel buried in the mountains of letters, the names of all those who died; I felt overwhelmed with a feeling of failure. I knew we had the responsibility to do the best, to return our best, and to return the soldiers to their families and loved ones, but somehow the truth was in my face.

Remember the sadness I spoke of as a child placing the flowers on the soldier's graves in Gettysburg? Well, here there were names and names and no graves. Knowing that I cared for so many young men who did not get home was a realization that hit me hard.

Several years later, in November of 1993, the Women's Vietnam Memorial was dedicated. This was the memorial statue dedicated to us that day, and Diane Carlson Evans was the founder. The memorial looks over the wall, giving the impression that we, the nurses, are still tending to the ones who lost their lives.

I went to the dedication to help put closure to the feelings that I had carried for so many years. It was a very emotional week. Soldiers who had served in Vietnam came from all over the United States to say welcome home and thank you. I never thought I needed to hear someone say thank you for a job I had done some twenty years before.

But there they were, holding signs up with the names of the nurses who took care of them, trying to find them, yelling their names, saying thank you's loud, cheering, and applause. The emotion was more than I can even express today.

It took twenty years for me to really open up. My husband didn't even know I got a Bronze Star, and he said, "Why didn't you tell me why?" I said, "My best friend didn't get the Bronze Star so why should I get one? They did the exact same thing I did."

I do have PTSD. I'm fortunate enough to be able to handle it. I know that besides sounds, smells can sometimes trigger PTSD.

I was thinking of the time when I first landed in Vietnam and exited the plane. Besides the oppressive heat and humidity, I remember this fish market type of smell, sort of like decaying fish wafting over the tarmac.

The other unique smell that I only associate with Vietnam is pseudomonas. Pseudomonas was something we smelled daily in the ICU because we left soldiers' wounds open; we had what they call delayed primary closures. When a soldier came in and got wounded, he went to the operating room; all of the wounds were cleaned, but they could not be closed because of tetanus.

And there are several different reasons, and they were all bacteria. So the wounds were open, but they were bandaged. So, every day we went in and we had to undo the bandages, irrigate the wound, and bandage them up. Then, three days later, they went back to surgery and they were subject to another round of debridement.

Debridement for treating a wound in the skin involves the nurses thoroughly cleaning the wound and removing all thickened skin, infected or dead tissue, dirt, and residual material from dressings. And then, if the wound looked healthy, the doctors would sew it up. Pseudomonas has a very strange, unique smell. It smells fruity, like grape juice, but has a slight mixture of a tortilla chip odor mixed in.

While at the wall, a Gold Star wife presented us with our 50-year commemorative pin. I tried to tell her that it's only been 45 years, but she explained that it's to be presented to any veteran who served anywhere in the armed forces from November 1, 1955, to May 15, 1975. I want to thank all those who supported our soldiers during those troubled times.

Thinking back about the war, I think of what I went through, and my experience coming home is minimal compared to our soldiers. I can't even believe what those young kids had to face when they came back because they didn't have a place to go to work. Who were they going to talk about this with? Nobody wanted to know anything, and even other veterans didn't want to talk about it. So it was a very, very difficult time for veterans like that.

My decision to join the Army Nurse Corps was the best career choice I ever made. Those two years were filled with life-changing experiences and growing an understanding of who I am.

I'm proud of the privilege of serving my country and the young men and women I got to know, and they will always hold a piece of my heart. I am a Vietnam veteran, a souvenir of that war, a part of history that some try to remember and some try to forget. Each veteran has their own story.

We, as veterans, ask people to remember our fallen veterans and comrades. It has been said that the nation that forgets its veterans will itself be forgotten.

—Ginny Dornheggen

★★★

Laura Hines Kern

My most pivotal moment in Vietnam as a nurse was my first day. I just jumped off the helicopter and walked into the medical facility with my bags, looking for my supervisor. The chief nurse and one of the doctors quickly approached me and ordered me into the operating room.

I had taken one step into the operating room, and they wheeled a soldier by me who was missing both of his legs; they were blown off. When you see the people before they've had surgery, it's not a clean thing that you're looking at. It's a real mess. And I think one of his arms was also blown off.

They had probably six IVs going into this guy and all hanging blood, and they had extra blood down below the stretcher on the gurney. At that moment, all of my senses were assaulted. There was the metallic smell of blood, the smell of burned flesh mixed with the smell of explosives that wafted in the air. I couldn't take my eyes off those ragged and raw bloody stumps where his legs used to be.

I don't remember seeing even his face ... I don't remember. I can picture this bloody mass in a uniform, and that's about all I can picture. I took a physical step backward and took a big, deep breath as I was shocked by this horrific image of unimaginable carnage. I can remember so vividly saying to myself, "Laura, if you don't get control of your emotions right this second, you are going to be of no good to anyone—end of story."

I stood there trembling and thinking, okay, this is going to be a whole year here that I will be doing this, and I've got to get control. I believe that is one of the reasons why I was able to separate my professionalism from my emotions. I genuinely think that that split-second decision I made that day truly saved me.

★★★

My name is Laura Hines Kern, and I was a Lieutenant in the US Army during the Vietnam War. My dad served in World War II, but he didn't talk much about it. As a kid, I remember always being interested in world history. My father and I used to sit and watch a great Navy TV show called "Victory At Sea" every Friday night, and I think that's when I first became slightly interested in the military.

After high school, I was in nursing school, and money for me was tight because I was paying all my own bills. One day, an Army nursing recruiter showed up, and when she told us that the student nurse program would pay us a monthly stipend, which was enough to cover my last year of school, I didn't think about it for even a second. I just raised my hand and volunteered. I clearly remember it was May of 1968 because it was the highest casualty rate of the Vietnam War that month when I joined.

We watched the body counts from the war on the news every night on TV. That was how they decided that the war was going to be shown to the American people as us winning due to the body counts of the enemy killed.

I remember seeing those, and of course, there were a lot of protests, but it was a real kind of a far-off thing. I won't lie about joining the military. It wasn't some altruistic thought of serving my country—nope, nothing like that. It was just about getting through nursing school, which was my means to an end. For some reason, I never thought about the dangers of joining the Army.

My military journey started at Fort Sam Houston. Well, the truth is, at first, I didn't take the training very seriously. None of us actually did. I was a little nervous about it, but it was a completely different way of life. The Army's way of life, saluting, marching, and rank system. I grew up in a very egalitarian family, and everybody was the same no matter who they were. And so then you had this really rigid rank structure in the Army, and that was a big change for me.

After that, I went to Fitzsimmons, which is in Colorado, for the operating room course there. Then, only a couple of weeks later, I was deployed to Vietnam.

I was in the airplane bathroom as we made our final approach to land in Vietnam. An announcement came over the plane's loudspeaker, and they said that our destination, the Bien Hoa Air Base, was currently being rocketed and mortared. They told us that when you exit the plane, if you hear incoming rockets, lay flat on the ground, face down on the tarmac, and we'll instruct you from then on.

And I'm sitting in this bathroom thinking, what have I gotten myself into? That was traumatic enough that I have never been in an airplane bathroom since. When I now fly, I always stay in my seat. That's like one of the strange lingering things from the war. I mean, it's not a big deal, but it just still sticks in my head.

The stench was unbelievable as we landed and exited the plane. This overpowering smell hit us—it was just like a mixture of garbage, rotting fish heads, and rice. Next, the humidity and temperature hit you. It was like hitting a brick wall. It was something that I had never felt before. Walking through heavy air was almost a physical feeling because it was so incredibly humid. It was August when I arrived, and the temperature and humidity were probably around one hundred degrees.

From the plane, they rushed us onto buses parked on the tarmac with protective chicken wire on the windows and doors. I was later told the chicken wire prevented grenades from being thrown into the buses.

I remember vividly when they got us off the buses and rushed us into the main terminal as all my senses were off the charts. The terminal also housed all the troops leaving to go home. And I remember hearing these strange noises as I entered.

It was the sounds of hundreds of soldiers doing those handshakes that seem go on forever. Slapping their hands up and back, pounding their fists together in a rhythmic secret ritual that only they know the meaning of.

They also looked sloppy compared to the rigid uniform codes I'd seen so far. They were all a little thinner than most of the newer troops. Maybe that's why I thought they looked a little sloppy: Their faded and tattered uniforms hung off them. But they weren't just leaner; they also gave off a feeling of edginess.

They were allowed to go home in their uniforms, while we nurses had to wear our dress uniforms. I was in stockings, a skirt, and high heels doing all this traveling. These guys were glad they were going home, but I think their underlying anger was because most of these guys were drafted. They didn't choose to go to Vietnam.

Besides the edginess, I also sensed something else surprising: they looked at us with what I perceived as pity. We were just starting our tour, having no idea of what was about to come, and they were getting on that plane to leave.

Bien Hoa's Air Base was a bustling place in South-Central Vietnam, about sixteen miles from Ho Chi Minh City. It was a hub for American, Australian, and New Zealand soldiers.

They were having water rationing at that point, and they gave us literally one eight-ounce cup of water when we got there. They said we could do whatever we wanted with it. We could drink it, take a bath with it, or brush our teeth. That was all we were getting, and I chose to bathe in it. That first leg of my journey to Vietnam was a nearly twenty-four-hour, emotional rollercoaster, exhausting trip.

The following day, I went out for breakfast, and when I came back, my luggage had been broken into. They took all my newly purchased clothes. I figured if I had to be in fatigues for a year, I would at least have nice, comfortable underwear underneath. They took it all and probably sold it on the black market.

So I felt angry right from the start because that happened to me. But there was nobody to complain to; they were bringing people in and shuffling others back out, and everything was in a hurry. I later reported to the chief nurse, who told me where I was going. Immediately, the Dustoff Huey helicopters came and picked me up.

It was my first time on a helicopter, and although you think you'd be scared to death, I thought it was exhilarating. We flew with the doors wide open; you could see everything below. At that time, Vietnam was probably one of the most beautiful countries I have ever seen. It was war-ravaged, but you didn't get that sense from being up in the air.

I ended up taking a lot of helicopter rides because I later got engaged to a helicopter pilot. On my little time off, I would go out riding with him and the troops. One time, we went up by Dien Bien Phu, where the last French battle took place right around 1954.

The French Colonial Corps fought the battle against the Viet Minh Communists serving under General Giap. In that battle, over eleven thousand French troops were captured. Two American pilots, James McGovern and Wallace Buford, were also killed in the fight. I was told that all of the dead soldiers were buried standing up, facing France.

But back to my journey. They flew us out to the 67th Evac Hospital in Qui Nhon. Nobody met me at the landing zone. I got off the helicopter and had to find the chief nurse and report in. They brought me to the operating room to report to the OR supervisor. I took one step over the threshold into that operating room, and that was when they wheeled that first guy by me. The one I talked about in the beginning of my story who had lost both of his legs.

My best friend Ginny Dornheggen and I always talk about how we could cope with all the insanity over there while many others struggled so badly. I really think it was that first case in Vietnam, that split-second decision I made to not let the moment overwhelm me, that saved me.

Working as a combat nurse, I loved to be tested, and I got hooked on the following adrenaline rush. My mantra was to embrace the chaos instead of fighting it. I wanted the most complex cases with the most demanding challenges. I got to think faster and move faster, and every day, I learned more. I was in my OR mode. It wasn't that I was not sympathetic to the guys. I always touched on an emotional and a personal level with the guys coming in, but the actual physicalness of the job was separate.

In Vietnam, we did and saw things the rest of the civilian world could never even come close to imagining. One time, an injured soldier came in with a head wound. And sometimes, with head wounds, you sit down, sometimes you stand up and work. I was sitting, and I asked Dr. Chavez what time it was because part of my job was to keep track of time. He said he couldn't see the clock from where he stood and worked.

And I remember bending down a bit and looking through this guy's head. Earlier, we had had to make the hole where the bullet went through his head a little bigger. So I looked through his head, which was at eye level with me, and I could see the clock. It said ten past three.

A quick story of how crazy life can be about a year later: I'm back in the US, assisting in surgery at Brooke Army Medical Center in Houston, Texas. We're going to put a plate in this previously injured soldier's head. We had to take out the bone flaps on some of the older head wounds because they would get infected, and you couldn't put the bone back in. They always had a significant defect in their skull, so we put plates in place to protect the skull.

So I was scrubbed in on one of those cases, and Dr. Chavez, the same surgeon I worked with in Vietnam, walked in. He studies the patient for a few moments, turns to me, and asks if I recognize this patient. I looked and said, "No, I don't." He said this is the guy where you looked through his head to see what time it was. So we knew that he had made it out alive, and miraculously, after that, all that the patient only had was some hearing loss and a limp.

But the truth is, we had no idea after most of the patients we treated left our hospital whether they had made it or not. I always tried to keep my professional walls up, but there was one case that I just struggled to deal with. There was one guy—young, maybe twenty—and he'd lost both his legs and arms. One arm was amputated above the elbow; one arm was below the elbow.

Taking off arms bothered me a lot more than taking off legs because legs I knew could be replaced, but arms you couldn't. Back in the seventies, there was no decent replacement for the complexity of a human hand. So that always bothered me more. I decided I would go over and talk with him afterward.

I think he was in the ICU, and he had a contraption that hung down from the bed frame we called a trapeze so that he could move himself in bed. He could hook his one arm, which still had an elbow around it, to move himself, to at least give him a drop of control. When I walked over to his bed, he was asleep, but something caught my eye. Taped onto that trapeze facing him was a picture of his brand-new baby. The baby was probably about three months old.

I just thank God he was asleep because I just started crying. I knew he would never be able to touch that child with his own hands. That probably was one of the most...I mean, it just tore my heart out to see that, to think he was going home to this beautiful baby. But it was too much for me. The right place for me was definitely in the operating room.

It's a very tense, high-stress environment that requires rapid split-second thinking. You have to make good decisions. I mean, I learned to make decisions in my head, pros and cons, and I still see a legal pad in my head with a line down the center, pros and cons. I can make almost instant decisions. And so far, I believe they're almost always good. So, not many people can stand that kind of stress. It's a very different working environment.

But on the other side, I could not have handled talking to these guys afterward; that would've killed me. I would never have been able to do that, ever. I was in an environment where I fit. I could take all of that myself, all of that stress and the blood and the gore that I could handle.

The nurses who worked on the floor saw the patients clean and wrapped up. They didn't see that; it was just the rawness I had to deal with in the operating room. But that was easier for me to deal with than talking with these guys. I couldn't have done that. I would've gone crazy.

So, I was pretty well insulated, but that was the reason I chose to work in the operating room. When I was a nursing student and just starting, there was a case of a guy who was in a motorcycle accident, and they closed up his wounds, which you don't do with dirty wounds. You have to leave them open to drain. So he developed Clostridium perfringens, which is gas-gangrene. They brought him into our hyperbaric chamber, and they had killed his liver with the anesthetic gases. They had destroyed his liver back in those days with the treatments available.

So, he was awake and under local anesthesia. I was at the top of this big two-story hyperbaric chamber while watching it during part of my student program. He's screaming inside the tank. It was so horrifying I almost fainted, and I could see everything that was happening to him. It was awful.

That's why I only want to work on patients asleep under anesthesia. If somebody has their arm ripped off, I can handle that as long as they're sleeping. So, I was in the right place. But that one guy, I will never forget that young kid with the picture of his baby. It was awful.

Nursing in the war wasn't all just sadness. There were a few extreme moments where I easily could have been killed. The single most dangerous time for me was when a guy came in with an unexploded grenade with the pin pulled lodged in his buttocks.

The surgeon I had a great working relationship with came up to me while I was standing at the scrub sink and said, "Laura, we've got this patient with an unexploded grenade. The grenade handle, which is the last thing keeping it from exploding, is still being held in place by tissue or something. You are young and don't have any family. All of our other surgeons are married and have kids, and your work is as good as any surgeon's. Can you come in and do this case with me and try to take this hand grenade out of this guy's buttocks?"

And I said, sure. I mean, I was up for anything really challenging. So they sandbagged the entire operating room inside and out. We had steel pots on our heads. I had flak jackets on the front and back. If this grenade had gone off, we were at ground zero; we would've been just blown to pieces.

I don't know why we went to all that trouble, but we did. So he and I went into the operating room together, and they brought the patient in and carefully turned him over. All of his clothing had been cut off of him in the ER, and he'd gone to X-ray, and that's where they'd seen this unexploded grenade.

So they flipped him over and we started operating on him. He took one cheek, and I took the other. We started exploring, and at the same second, we both looked up at one another and said that the grenade was not there. We both tried to think: Where is it if it's not here? It's in his clothes!

They had taken the stretcher he was on—luckily, they just left it as it was. They had just pushed it because they had a mass casualty event that day with dozens of injured, they then moved the stretcher into the X-ray department. So we sent a message out very quickly to X-ray the empty stretcher , and there was the live grenade; the coagulated blood around it was holding it together.

They called in an EOD unit that handles unexploded ordinance and they took this grenade out, then exploded it in one of the little truck things that they had. So it was a live grenade, and it would've gone off. So that was probably the most harrowing yet exciting day I'd ever had.

But here's the kicker on that story. That surgeon, Dr. Wayne Dickerson, was his name. I loved him; watching him work was like watching a symphony. So, years later, in 1996, my husband and I moved to a small town in Washington state. One day, while driving, I passed a plastic surgeon's office and just happened to read the name on the sign, Dr. Wayne Dickerson.

I immediately stopped and went in; believe it or not, it was the same surgeon I worked with on the other side of the world almost twenty-five years earlier. It was great seeing him, and we talked about that one episode with the hand grenade. He's died since then, but what a great man and surgeon.

The grenade incident wasn't the only strange occurrence in our hospital. One guy, a US soldier, got shot in the heart while playing poker with his buddies, and they rushed him into us. Not that we could do anything. We didn't have the proper equipment to work on hearts. I think they investigated it, and it was people in his company. They accused him of cheating or something, and somebody just pulled out a gun and shot him, just crazy.

There was this other time when one young, injured soldier was parked out in the hallway near the operating room. He called me over, and I asked, "What's the issue?" He said, "I don't know what I'm going to tell my girlfriend." I said, "Well, what are you talking about?" And I looked up, and the top part of his scalp was gone.

The whole center portion of his scalp, straight on the top of his head, was missing, and it was down to the bone, and that's what we were going to be cleaning out and repairing.

I said, "Well, tell me what happened." He had dropped a rocket into a rocket launcher, and it didn't come out. So he put his head down in front of it to see if it was still in there. Of course, right at the moment, it shot out, and the fins took off the top part of his scalp.

So he's telling me this story, and I said, "Well, soldier, let me tell you one thing: If you tell her the truth, it's so stupid she will probably never go out with you again." I said, "We're going to make up a story right now about how you got wounded, and that's what you're going to tell her." We made up some kind of a great story that he loved, and he felt relieved.

We obviously treated a lot of gunshot wounds to the abdomen. Those cases can be tricky because sometimes the bullet only makes a tiny little hole going in. So if the bullet doesn't come out, it's somewhere in there, but it kind of tears up the bowel, and you have to run the bowel, which means go over every single inch to see if there are any holes. You can't have bowels leaking into the abdomen.

So, we have to visually inspect it with our eyes and then feel the entire bowel with our fingers. It's sort of like a ribbon. You pull it out and lay it on their abdomen, then you flip it over to look at the other side, checking for holes. It's attached to the body with the omentum. The omentum is a large, flat adipose tissue layer that hangs down from the greater curve of the stomach, floating on the surface of the small and large bowels. In layman's terms, it looks like a lace structure that holds the bowels in place.

After you're satisfied there are no holes, you basically just kind of lay it back in, or sometimes you have to kind of stuff it back in there. Then, lots of times, we'd have to pick up the sides of the incision, and you just kind of bounce the abdomen around a little bit. It's like if you had a saltshaker that was too full, and you just banged it a little bit to get more salt in.

One day, there was this really, really difficult decision I had to make. It was one of the days I was in charge of the operating room and triage. There was this young civilian girl—I think four or five years old—that was brought in with a severe head wound. At the time, we were receiving mass casualties from a nearby battle. I think three of the US soldiers had severe head wounds, and we had only two neurosurgeons.

One of the neurosurgeons bypassed me and went to another ER doctor and said he wanted to work on this baby girl first before the US soldiers. I said, no, we treat our critical men first; that was our mission. The neurosurgeon argued with me, and another neurosurgeon came over to us and said that, basically, this little girl was just about dead and had a low probability of surviving regardless.

We all went to work and we got all of the major surgeries done: one surgeon says the baby's dead, another surgeon says, no, the baby's alive. So we brought her in and worked on her, I don't know, for two hours. Sadly, no matter how hard we worked, she just died on the table.

Afterwards, I was standing there washing this little lifeless child to put her in a body bag. It was my responsibility to perform that final act. We had to return her to her family. We had worked so hard to save her life but we couldn't save everyone, and that's what war really is.

But for all those ugly, tragic cases, Vietnam honed my nursing capabilities to a fine degree. There was nothing I couldn't do or handle when it came to treating complex injuries. So, thousands of people benefited back home from the experiences I learned there. And that's where we honed the Dustoff system with helicopters, which is now utilized by all our first responders here in the US.

I also want to mention that working in high-stress environments sometimes requires you to do some stuff to blow off steam. Two Navy guys visited Ginny and me one day, and we had nothing else to do. So we decided the chief nurse"—the head of all the nurses—and a full colonel needed a surprise. When she went into her room to take a nap, we sandbagged her.

All of our camp doors opened outward, so I decided it would be fun to sandbag her in her room. Ginny was too chicken to help out. She wasn't like me, and she didn't make any waves. Ginny said, "I'll just be the lookout and tell you if anybody comes." So the three of us took sandbags from outside the building and piled them up in front of her door, and we could hear her when she got up banging on the door for somebody to please let her out.

Nobody would let her out, and they never found out who had done it. About six months later, when I had already gone home, there was a big newspaper article about trying to figure out who had sandbagged Colonel Lafferty in her room. They never found out, and now I'm finally admitting it. It was me. It's funny how things change because now I'm a real rule-follower. I don't do anything dangerous or against the laws or the rules. But back then, it was just a whole different ball game.

People have asked me if I'd wanted to stay longer in Vietnam. Well, even though I loved the challenges, I did want to leave. There was no question in my mind that I wanted to leave. I had a younger brother—four years younger than I was—and he was getting out of high school.

We didn't know whether or not he was going to go to college. I called my mother to find out my brother's draft number. I needed to know what his lottery number was because if his lottery number was low—say his birthday came up as lottery number seventeen— he'd be guaranteed to go to Vietnam. I would stay an extra year if that was the case.

Because of the rules of siblings not serving at the same time, I would stay another year or two to protect my younger brother from coming here. I didn't want him walking in those jungles. No, not my little brother. But his lottery number was very high, so I didn't end up having to stay. To this day, he still blames me in a joking-around kind of way.

I knew the exact date I was going to leave. We had what we called a short-timers calendar, and mine hung up in the operating room. For your last month there, you crossed off the days, every day. You were called a short-timer, meaning your time was short there. And so my DEROS—date of estimated rotation of service— was on the exact day I'd arrived in Vietnam a year before.

That day finally came. I remember when we were about to board the plane, they were checking us for drugs because there was a huge drug issue at that time. The plane maybe held about two hundred, fifty people. So they brought the enlisted people out first, and they frisked them. They lined them up out on the tarmac in three lines.

And then they took all of the officers and they made a U-shape kind of a wall around them as they were frisking us so that the enlisted people could not go anywhere—either to get drugs or do drugs or whatever. And they frisked all of us.

I was the only woman on board, and the guy was kind of tired when he came to me and started his search. Suddenly, he realized that it was a woman he was frisking. I heard him say, "What do I do now?" And I said, "Just frisk me. I just want to get on that plane. I don't care."

When we finally got on the plane and were seated, and it was dead silent. And as we took off down that runway, even to this day, it's just very emotional for me to even think about it because there was absolutely no talking or noise.

As we lifted off and those wheels came up into that airplane, all of these men who had been out in the field and who had been shot at, who had been just in miserable conditions for a whole year, they let out this just base guttural roar. It was a visceral roar that exploded throughout the cabin. The roar of relief that they were finally going home in one piece.

I felt it, too, but not like these men felt it. I mean, if you have to pick from one to ten how much danger your life was in, their lives were up around a ten in constant danger. Mine was probably at a four. So, I didn't have that constant pressure of thinking that I was going to be killed. But these poor guys were just so glad to be going home alive. Unless you experienced something like that, you can't understand. It is a moment I will never, ever, ever forget.

I came back in August 1971, and I wanted to mention that although you may leave Vietnam, Vietnam never leaves you. Numerous times while I was back in the States, parts of the war would come back into my life, not just in a bad way but also sometimes in a good way.

There was this one soldier I treated in Vietnam, and the only reason I remembered treating him was because he was brought in wounded, wrapped with these perfectly white sheets. Now, there were no white sheets over there. All of our sheets were that Army blue, or gray in color. The operating room and the hospital had no white sheets at all. I don't know where these white sheets came from, but he had white sheets on when he came in from his unit. We talked for a while before he went into surgery.

He called me, I think, right around 1972, to thank me. He was at Fort Sam Houston recuperating, and he found me there. We just said a quick hello, and that was about it. Fast forward to 1993, and I'm at the Women's Memorial dedication. We had our own hospital banner posted, and we were under it in a little booth.

This guy walked up to our banner and said across the board, "I'm looking for the nurse who took care of me. I came in with white sheets on." I went, whoa, that was me he was looking for. He said he had thought about it every day of his life. He just wanted to come in and thank the nurse who took care of him. So he did. And that was the last time I ever heard from him, but it made me feel great.

Another interesting story happened to me while working as a volunteer nurse in Washington. I was walking by the operating room and they were waking a patient up from surgery. I could hear a lot of screaming and yelling going on, so I peeked my head in and looked: this enormous man was on the table.

I knew he was well over six feet tall because we had to put an extension on the table for their feet when people were that big. There were eight people standing around him trying to hold him down, and he was lifting all the people off of the floor. Everyone was screaming. They could not get control of him. He was waking up from anesthesia and screaming. So I walked in and recognized what he was calling out and shouting: he was calling out artillery coordinates.

I said, "What's his name?" I think they said his name was Ed. And I walked up to him. Now he's lifting all these people up and just going wild. I walked up and I started talking to him precisely as I would speak to soldiers in Vietnam when they came in. The same tone of voice and the same cadence I knew they were used to. As soon as I started talking to him, he relaxed like a baby on that table.

He became perfectly still and everyone looked at me wide-eyed. What in the world have you just done? No one could understand what was going on. They said, "Just keep talking to him."

I went back to talk with him after he woke up fully from the anesthesia he had been under. I said, "Were you in Vietnam?" He said yes. And I asked, "What years were you there?" He said 1970 to 1971; the exact years I was there. I asked, "Where were you?" and he said, right outside of Quin Nhon; the same place I was in.

I talked to him a little bit and found out he had been wounded three times while he was over there. I later spoke to a doctor in charge of anesthesia and explained to him what happened. I asked him about the patient's immediate response to my voice, and he said, "Laura, you must have taken care of him while he was in Vietnam, and his subconscious recognized your voice." Now that's pretty wild!"

—Laura Hines Kern

★★★

"To be 'in charge' is certainly not only to carry out the proper measures yourself, but to see that everyone else does so too."

— Florence Nightingale

Maureen Robinson

Authors note: I came across Nurse Robinson's story while researching information about the 27th Surgical Hospital. Ms. Robinson wrote an open letter asking for help to locate a Vietnam War "Dustoff" helicopter crew.

To become a decent writer, you must be an avid reader and love discovering well-written, moving stories. Nurse Robinson's letter below exemplifies a unique, heart-wrenching tale written by a humble heroine. It took me a few weeks to track her down, and she generously agreed to allow me to interview her for this book. The following is her letter, slightly edited for flow, followed by my phone interview.

★ ★ ★

My name is Maureen Robinson. I was a Captain in the US Army Nurse Corps stationed at the 27th Surgical Hospital in Chu Lai from April 1970 to May 1971.

This story is dedicated to my son Dinh Nit (Mark), a member of the Hre' Tribe (pronounced "Ray"), and to all Montagnards everywhere who continue to struggle for the basic human rights that are denied to them. The Montagnards are a mixed ethnic group that inhabit the highland areas of Vietnam.

I hope that by telling our story, someone may recall something that will help to piece together the first three years of my son's life. I was attached to the 24th Evac in Long Binh during my first tour in Vietnam and was discharged in early 1968. I then worked in orthopedics at Walter Reed Hospital. I never forgot my time in Vietnam and was ready to return in late 1969.

Initially, I was going to return as a civilian. I interviewed with Catholic Charities and also considered a plastic surgery hospital in Saigon. Then the Army came up with an offer I couldn't refuse: a thirteen-month tour for former army nurses who were Vietnam vets. So, by April 1970, I was on my way.

My assignment was the emergency room, but I guess you could say that a twist of fate had me working on the wards set up for civilian casualties and ARVN soldiers. That temporary assignment turned into a permanent one by choice.

Our patients ranged from premature babies to geriatrics, and we cared for the casualties of war, traumatic amputations, fractures, shrapnel wounds, burns, and all the after-effects of mines and weapons. We were also challenged by tropical diseases—too many to mention, but malaria, blackwater fever, scrub typhus, and dengue fever were a few. Then, there were assorted medical problems, including severe cases of malnutrition. Many of our patients were children, and sometimes they were beyond our help.

The staff tried very hard to do their best under challenging conditions. I can't name them all, but Captain Grace Squires was the head nurse and very dedicated to her patients. There were good and bad times, funny and sad, and I will never forget the staff of Wards Five and Six.

Time passed, and we were busy, with a few lulls along the way. There had been an increase in activity, and we had the usual alerts. Then, at the beginning of November, the nurses' quarters were destroyed by fire. We were moved to two unoccupied wards used for storage. Most of us lost just about everything.

The EMs rushed to try and salvage what they could for us, but I can still remember seeing my "smoking" jungle boots thrown over the side. For the next few days, I worked wearing flip-flops and a uniform two sizes too big. I had to improvise with a belt to hold it all together. I guess it provided some comedy relief for all.

The nurses at the 91st Evac Hospital donated clothes to help us out. I was upset that all of the clothes that I had obtained for the kids were destroyed in the fire.

About a week later, the twist of fate that found me assigned to my unit was about to take another turn. I remember that evening on the 8th of November, 1970, like it was yesterday. I walked into the ward and saw a new patient.

His record stated that he was about three years old and picked up by a Dustoff helicopter in the Tra Bong District. His name was Dinh Nit, and he was suffering from severe malnutrition and several infections. His muscle tone was so poor that even basic food digestion was difficult for him.

His abdomen was swollen from parasite infections and protein deficiency, and he weighed only eighteen pounds. There was a young boy with him who said he was his brother and fifteen. He appeared to be no more than twelve. I remember he wore the tiger stripe fatigues common to PF and Montagnards attached to SF. After a couple of days, he left, and word was that he had to get back. I never saw him again.

During the weeks that followed, Dinh Nit thrived. He gained weight, and his infections responded to treatment. He picked up English and Vietnamese, and I became increasingly attached to this little guy. I can't say the exact moment I decided to adopt him, but I remember the day I asked him if he wanted to be my son and go to America.

He asked me if there were bunkers in America. When I said no, he looked very surprised and said, "What you do when Viet Cong come?" This was the world as he knew it: the VC and the war. He, like so many others, could not imagine any other life.

Time passed too quickly, and I was due in April 1971 at DEROS (date estimated return overseas). I put in for an extension and began the one step forward and ten backward which would be our story for the next nine months.

It is too involved to cover here, but I will relate a few incidents along the way. I met Lt. Steve Thayer, Civil Service, who would be instrumental in helping us through the tough days that lay ahead. He arranged for our trips to Tra Bong and provided Sgt. Minh to interpret and help me through the adoption process. He would be Nit's godfather.

My DEROS date was nearing, and no word was coming regarding approval. Whenever Col. Fore, the chief nurse, would ask me about it, I just said the paperwork was due anytime. In reality, I didn't have a clue, but Plan A was to keep reporting for duty. There was no Plan B. On the day that was to be my DEROS date, I arrived at the unit and was told that Colonel Fore wanted to see me. That was the longest walk I ever took.

I was thinking of a plan that would permit me to stay and keep Nit from being placed in an orphanage. Col. Fore looked at me and said, "Your extension came through this morning." I knew that we were on borrowed time. If things didn't look promising, Nit would be discharged to an orphanage.

There was an increase in enemy activity around this time, and one night, the US Navy fired into the mountains that were just across from the 27th. For some reason, the 27th Surgical Hospital was situated in front of the American Headquarters and other units. Artillery Hill was just across Highway One from us, and the Australians had turned it over to the Army of the Republic of Vietnam (ARVN).

I was on duty that evening and remember when the first round hit. Somehow, the 27th was not informed of the plan, so we were all caught by surprise. The ground shook, and everything seemed to be in double. We scrambled to get the patients who could be moved under the beds and cover the ones who couldn't be moved with any protection we could find.

Dinh Nit and Dinh Duong spent that night under the nurse's station wearing our helmets. The Viet Cong managed a few rounds of their own, but no damage was done.

We made several trips to Tra Bong to get permission from the District Chief to adopt. I remember flying in a chopper and following a dry riverbed to the mountains and Tra Bong. There was a Special Forces base camp, and I remember an airstrip of sorts from where the C130s landed. There was a small waterfall coming down the side of a mountain, and in the valley below were rice paddies.

The district headquarters showed signs of a previous attack by the VC. There were large shell holes in the buildings. There were hamlets up on the mountainside, and I also remember seeing Montagnard's homes. I managed my visits in my off time and never really asked permission to go to the mountains. I think I sensed what the answer would be, so it was a case of no one asking, and I didn't tell. I was told that I would have to bring Dinh Nit to Tra Bong per the order of the district chief. I was hesitant for apparent reasons but felt there was no choice.

On this trip, a long line of Montagnards was waiting to see if Nit was the son, brother, nephew, etc., that each sought. It was sad. One Montagnard arrived with his crossbow over his shoulder and wearing only a loincloth.

He lifted Nit's shirt to look for signs of a bullet wound. He was desperately trying to find his nephew. He shook his head no and looked directly at me, then nodded as if to say take care of this child. Nit was very quiet during this whole period. He was not afraid but, I think, somewhat overwhelmed by the experience.

On one trip, our flight was canceled due to the weather and we had to spend the night. I managed to get a call through to Grace Squires to cover for me. Thankfully, my shift the next day didn't start until 1900. They were expecting a visit from "Charlie," the enemy, and we were told what to do if that happened. Artillery fired all night and every time a round went off, Nit would roll over, and at one point, he fell out of bed.

He was the only casualty that night, suffering a black eye. The next morning, we were on our way. The chopper crew had to pick up and deliver ammo, so we were dropped on a hilltop "somewhere" and picked up about a half hour later.

There was a camp down a dirt road and a platoon came in from the bush. They looked so tired and beat. I am not sure what they thought about passing a young Montagnard boy and an Army nurse sitting on a hilltop just down from their base camp.

After dozens of heart-wrenching setbacks, I finally received permission to adopt Nit. The next hurdle was to process the adoption and obtain a visa. Vietnamese law states one has to be married and at least thirty. I was single and twenty-six.

The orphanage in An Thon recommended Star of the Sea Orphanage in Da Nang. They handled adoptions for the US and Europe. I found an attorney who was affiliated with the orphanage, and she agreed to help us. This was just the beginning of our arduous journey.

The 27th Hospital was due to close, and we all received new assignments. I got assigned to the 91st Evac Hospital, about five miles away. At first, I was told that Nit would have to be placed in an orphanage until the adoption was finalized. But I pleaded my case and at the eleventh hour, the chief nurse of the 91st agreed that he could come with me. I don't think many thought that we would be successful. Again, I was told if the adoption did not go through, Nit would be discharged to an orphanage. In May 1971, we finally moved.

On our first night, there was an alert and we spent some time in the bunker. Nit slept through it all. I was assigned to Ward Four and my duties were to continue to care for civilian and ARVN casualties. There was also a section for prisoners of war casualties. I would bring Nit to work and he would play with the kids there.

When I worked the night shift 1900–0700 hours, Nit slept on the ward, and usually, one of the nurses would keep an eye out for him so that I could get a few hours of sleep. They were all a dedicated group and I was glad to have the opportunity to serve with them. This was the ward that Lt. Sharon Lane worked on. She was the nurse killed in a rocket attack in 1969.

I had put in for another three-month extension as the "ten-steps backward, one-step forward" routine was still going strong. Then, one June morning, while on duty, Steve Thayer called me. He asked me how it felt to be a mother. I was a little slow on the uptake, but when it sunk in, I was ecstatic. Finally, thanks to help from so many individuals and a lot of prayers, Dinh Nit was officially my son!

I named him Mark Stephen, and his birth date was recorded as November 8th, the day he arrived at our hospital. He would keep his Montagnard name when confirmed at age nine.

The visa would prove to be another hurdle, and Steve Thayer was getting ready to return to the United States. While still at the 27th, Nit and I had to travel to Saigon—about four hundred miles south—to apply for a visa at the American Embassy. I remember that one of the corpsmen stood in for me at the airport on standby so I could catch a few hours of sleep after night duty.

As we left the 27th, Colonel Fore, the executive officer, and other 27th staff stood and wished us luck. I had received a three-day pass to cover the trip. The executive officer gave me a number to call if we had problems returning. It would prove to be a lifesaver.

We stayed at the Third Field Hospital in Saigon. I filled out the paperwork at the embassy and was told that a number had been assigned, but they could not tell me when he would be able to receive his visa. All numbers came by way of Manila.

I contacted an attorney in Saigon, but the Catholic orphanage that he worked with insisted that Nit would have to remain there. I wasn't about to leave him 400 miles from where I was stationed.

The push was on in Cambodia and all flights north were pretty much diverted. I called the number given to me and was given a list of courier flights that would prove to be our "hitchhiking" way back to Chu Lai. I could not tell you where we traveled that day in

Vietnam: We would board one chopper, then be dropped off in a clearing "somewhere" and another would arrive and pick us up. That was pretty much our day, and Nit, as always, was a real trooper through it all.

Finally, I was notified that his number had arrived, but I would have to travel to Saigon to pick up the visa. Jack Litzmann, one of the corpsmen, was going to Saigon and volunteered to go to the embassy. Everything was starting to fall into place.

In late September, Nit and I were getting ready to leave. I had mixed feelings. So much had happened in the seventeen months that I'd spent there, and I knew that this would be a final farewell. It was hard to say goodbye to all the friends we'd made. Nit was almost four now, and he knew we were going on a long trip, but I also knew that he would be leaving a way of life and beginning a new one. It was a gigantic step for one so young and innocent.

We said our tearful goodbyes and arrived in Cam Ranh Bay, but the latest problem was that Nit had to leave Saigon. So the following day, at 0400 hours, we were on another flight to Saigon. We spent a couple of days at Camp Alpha while I tried to get a flight to the US.

One sergeant told me that there were no seats available for two weeks. After I said that we would sit on the floor of the plane—or whatever it took—he told me not to worry and got us a spot on a flight the next day. When we were going through customs, the Air Force sergeant commented, "Wow, you just made it." I shockingly realized that this was the last day for Nit's visa to be valid.

The Vietnamese guard was the last step, the last obstacle before getting on the plane, and they looked at Nit's passport over and over with intense scrutiny. My nerves were shot as I thought, how could we have traveled so far, overcome so much adversity to be denied at the last moment? The seconds seemed to tick on forever, and then, finally, he slowly looked up, smiled, and waved us on. What once seemed to be impossible was finally coming true.

Today, Mark is the father of Kathy, Stephen, and Jason. He met his wife Ling in Pittsburgh while attending university. He and his wife currently run their own restaurant.

Mark grew up in Chester, PA, which is not far from Philadelphia. He was a popular kid, and my claim to fame was that I was known as Mark's mom. My parents were devoted to their new grandson, and each of them influenced him during his childhood. It was love at first sight.

He excelled at sports in school, and as one neighbor stated, "That boy can run like the wind." Thinking back to his arrival at the 27th, it was quite a remarkable recovery. Now, he passes on his story to his children. The boys hear bedtime stories of their dad in Vietnam and the Montagnards.

I am proud of my son for many things, but mostly because he is a decent man and devoted to his family. His parents in Vietnam would have been proud of him. He is a good man.

I would like to relate one more short story. When Mark was about seven, I passed by his room and he asked me how to spell Montagnard. I asked him what he was writing, and he said he was composing a letter to his mother in Viet Nam.

This was around the time things were going from bad to worse there. This is what I remember—the original I gave to Mark a couple of years ago.

Dear Mom,

I hope that you are well. I am fine. I have a new family now and am happy. I am sad that the VC are fighting the Montagnards. I hope that you are OK. We will win. We are Montagnards and a proud people.

Love,

It was a very poignant letter, and he asked me to mail it. I didn't know what to say, but I kept it and gave it to him years later. The Hre's spirit lives on in my son and will be passed on to his children. That is the way it should be.

I am trying to locate the Dustoff crew that picked up my son in Tra Bong or the ground unit that put him on board on November 8, 1970. He was about three at the time and a member of the Hre' Tribe. It was a morning/afternoon mission.

Mark (Dinh Nit) was suffering from severe malnutrition and several infections. A young boy with him said he was his brother and fifteen. He appeared to be no more than twelve. I remember that he wore tiger stripe fatigues, which are common with PF and Montagnards attached to Special Forces. After a few days, the boy left. Word was that he had to get back. I never saw him again.

—Maureen Robinson.

27th Surg Hospital, Chu Lai, 1970

Maureen Robinson: Mark adapted readily to coming to the States. There was instant love between him and his grandparents. I mean, they just loved him to death. And my sister. He made friends easily. He was not shy; he was very personable and everybody knew him.

When he started school, he did very well. He loved sports. And when I think about how sick he was when he was first admitted, and the doctor said, "He will always be sick. Are you sure you want to adopt? He's not going to be a healthy kid."

I guess it was about the fifth grade when Mark got into school. He wanted to try out for the local football team, but he was not really big. And I thought, but I can't say *no, you can't because you're not going to get in because you're smaller.* Well, he did get on the team, and he was a running back, and everybody got to know him because he was really very good.

Mark was the only Asian in school and the only Asian in the neighborhood at the time. So constantly, people would ask him where he was from, and he would tell them, but they didn't understand what a Montagnard is. I said, "Well, you have to tell them all about your people. Hold your head high and be proud you're a Montagnard." I know at times it probably wasn't easy, but Mark got along with everybody.

Mark Dinh Nit Robinson said this: I just felt like I was one of the kids. There was for me no difference of me being Asian and them being white or black. There were very few people of color in our school, but I've never felt that I was out of place, even at that young age. There was a sense of brotherhood among everybody.

I loved playing football because I felt it was an opportunity to show people what I love to do. Football gave me a very good sense of teamwork and sacrifice. I always thought organized sports was quintessential Americana. Looking back now, I really believe that is how Americans are. I think that's how Montagnards are as well, where you got each others' backs, and you fight for one another.

Author David Yuzuk phone interview: *Thank you, Ms. Robinson, for taking the time to talk to me. The thing about your story that's so harrowing is that so many times, it could have easily ended. So many times, you're so close to getting him adopted, getting him home, getting him on planes, and then you are almost stopped. Thank God it worked out the way it did, but it certainly seemed very nerve-racking and precarious.*

Maureen Robinson (MR): It was! It was like one step forward and ten back, and there were so many different people who came along on the way. Either that helped in a small way or a huge way. It just seemed like when I needed that particular help, it came, and we would've not made it had it not been for all those people along the way, both Vietnamese and American; it all came together.

I really hope that we find out who the Dustoff crew was. The ones who picked up Mark.

MR: Well, I tried that. That's why I initially put that website up: the guy who had that website lives in England. He's French, but he lives in England, and he was interested in Special Forces in Vietnam during the War. He's the one who suggested that I could write something up and then include some photos and just maybe somebody seeing it.

Well, through the years, I mean, different people have contacted me, but we never quite found anyone. And I can understand that it really was trying to find a needle in the haystack because I mean, they flew missions all the time and just try to remember one mission out of many, it's almost like impossible on top of it.

So you didn't have any contact with that Dustoff crew? Somebody just brought Mark in, and you heard he came in with a Dustoff crew?

MR: Yeah, it was on his record that he had come in prior to him arriving. I'm trying to think maybe about a week before he came to the hospital. Our nurse's quarters burned down, so we were put in an empty ward right across from where I worked. And I just remember walking in that evening, and I usually say I worked on taking care of wounded and medically ill Vietnamese civilians and Montagnards.

There were some ARVN soldiers, too, and when I would walk on, there'd be a lot of kids, and I'd go, hi, just talk to them or smile or wave. And I said to this one group of kids, hi, how are you? And this little voice came back, hi, how are you? And it was Mark, and it was the first time that I met him. I opted for his birthday to be the day he arrived at the hospital November 8, 1970. That's how he got his birthday.

Mark spoke English?

MR: He repeated what I said; kids could pick it up in a heartbeat, like little sponges. They would pick up phrases, which are not sometimes the best words to pick up. Mark wasn't fluent in English, but he liked what I said and repeated it. Many of the "Yards" seemed to have had the ability to quickly pick up our words and accents.

And when I say "Yards," or Montagnards, that's what the French originally used as the name for the people who live in the hills. Montagnards were like our Native Americans here. They had many different tribes. Each tribe had its own language, its own customs, etcetera. But I say Montagnards in general. And the American soldiers used to call them "Yards."

How long do you think after the Dustoff crew brought him in that you actually met him? Was he there for a day or so? And how old was he?

MR: I think he was there for a day or a little less before I met him. The Montagnards didn't keep what we recognize as a birth record. You were born during the harvest season, the rainy season, etcetera. So they estimated that Mark was around three years old.

At the time I met him, he only weighed eighteen pounds and had a huge, distorted belly. His feet were swollen and his hands were puffy. He didn't have much hair on his head and he had a lot of problems with parasites, bronchitis, ear infection—just various things that were wrong with him.

He was recorded as being picked up in Quang Ngai, and that's way up in the hills, in the Central Highlands. It was a remote area, but within maybe a five to seven-mile radius. There were several US Special Forces base camps in that area.

Many of the Montagnards would work with special forces as Scouts and would go on patrols. And where he was picked up, this wasn't like a big pickup section. When I went there, the runway was a dirt road essentially covered by these big steel mats.

What was he wearing when you first met him?

MR: He had a little white but faded shirt and probably a short pair of pants. We used to keep a lot from donations. We could keep clothes on the ward. The Montagnards didn't always wear tribal dress. Sometimes, they would wear a shirt, usually in the old times, and not very much today at all. The men and young boys would wear loincloths. And they would, depending on their tribe, wear a necklace.

They always had a brass wrist bracelet, sometimes a necklace. Mark came in with a small bracelet on his ankle. One day, he took it off his ankle, handed it to me, and said, "Here, you keep it. I'm not baby anymore."

Because he was so sick, he had accompanying him a young boy who looked to me to be about twelve years old. Through an interpreter, he said he carried Mark to the camp, and he was his brother. He wore these tiger stripe fatigues, which some of the Montagnards would wear as part of the popular force in that area. And I knew that boy was working with an American unit by wearing that outfit.

The boy only stayed for two or three days. One day, he was just gone. I got the message that he had to get back to his people. How he got back, I will never know because where Mark came from, the way I would get there, would be by chopper. They had to follow this dry riverbed up in the mountains, and that area was the territory of the Viet Cong.

So you think the scenario is that Mark's family believed that he's too sick, so they told the 15-year-old kid to bring him to the American soldiers, the special forces guys, and see if they can get him some sort of treatment?

MR: Well, it could be. This is where I really don't have a lot of information. It could have been the Special Forces because they would sometimes send kids or people in who they felt needed extra medical attention. My guess is, with Mark and the condition he was in, either his mother was dead or possibly very ill, or there might've been another younger child that needed more attention.

When Mark was a child, did he ever ask you to take him back to Vietnam?

MR: I remember the time when we were pulling out of Vietnam, when Saigon was falling and everything was on the TV all the time. I asked him once if he would like to go back to Vietnam to visit. He was only about eight or nine. And he shook his head no. And I asked why not? He goes, "Because they will shoot me."

I did take him to North Carolina to meet with other Montagnards. I guess back in the late eighties and early nineties, US Special Forces soldiers decided they were going to help try to get the Montagnards to the States.

Every Special Forces soldier I spoke to who worked with the Montagnards told me they were the bravest and most loyal fighters they ever worked with. I guess there was a very strong bond between SF soldiers and the "Yards," especially the Green Berets who worked with them the most.

After the war, the Montagnards were being killed by the communists. Several hundred Montagnards made their way to a refugee camp in Thailand. The North Vietnamese Army was destroying all these Montagnard villages and everyone in them.

I don't know how many died that way, but some made their way to Cambodia. For close to thirty years, they survived in the jungles of Cambodia; they learned what plants were dangerous and which plants would help to heal.

The Special Forces soldiers went to Thailand and helped them get to North Carolina. The Montagnards eventually bought this land in the Smoky Mountains, which kind of resembled the Central Highlands, with the trees and the river nearby. They make it like a community, a center for meetings and reunions.

We were down there maybe ten years ago, and I had never seen Mark smile so much. I think he smiled the entire day. That's the first time he was among so many Montagnards since Vietnam. But nobody from his original tribe was there, which was very sad. I tried to do my best over the years to support my son and be the best mom I could because he was the best son a mother could ever ask for!

Sources: Materials USVeteranslegacy.org interview.

Diane Carlson Evans

One night that I vividly remember was when we were rocketed and mortared. Your training just kicks in. You grab your helmet and flak jacket because if you get hit, what good are you to your patients?

Soon, the red alert siren went off. We then heard the incoming, and shrapnel was flying around; that's when the standard operating procedure [SOP] kicked in: get your patients under the bed. Well, we didn't have to tell our patients to get under the bed. They were already under the bed. They woke up like that, hitting the ground or the jungle. You do what it takes to survive.

But now they've pulled out their bloodlines. They've pulled out their IVs. We do have extensions, if they ever have to get under the beds. So now I've got one guy, the bloodline, he's pulled that out, and there's blood everywhere. So I get his bloodline back together. He's now under the bed. And then we throw mattresses on the tops of the guys who have trachs and chest tubes and can't get under the bed.

So, I'm throwing mattresses on. There's one other military nurse with me and two medics, and we're just doing everything we can to protect them in the best way that we can. But the little girl in the unit—we were caring for Vietnamese civilians and children who were injured in the crossfires of the war—she had a napalm burn. And I say this because that little girl came into our unit screaming in pain, and when we got hit, she started screaming because it scared her. Like the night her village was bombed and she started screaming. I couldn't throw a mattress on top of her. She was badly burned. I went under her crib, and I just held her hand, and she screamed herself to death...

Diane Carlson Evans is a remarkable figure in American history. Her journey from the battlefields of Vietnam to the halls of advocacy illustrates the profound impact that one individual can have.

Evans was born in 1946 and raised on a dairy farm in rural Minnesota. Her aunt served in the Women's Army Corps during World War II, her oldest brother joined the Army, and her other brother served in Vietnam.

In 1966, Evans met with a military nurse recruiter while attending nursing school. She joined a program in which she received a stipend for school in exchange for two years of military service.

On August 1, 1968, at only twenty-one years old, Evans arrived in Vietnam as a member of the 36th Evacuation Hospital. She worked twelve- to fourteen-hour shifts in understaffed, 105-degree Quonset huts treating burn victims. But Evans requested a transfer north, where there was more active combat. She became head nurse of the 71st Evacuation Hospital in Pleiku, located near the Cambodian border.

The hospital was constantly under fire and the wounded came in waves directly from the battlefield. Evans learned to focus on her patients instead of the chaos around her to provide the best care. She protected them during an incoming attack before taking shelter herself. After leaving Vietnam, Evans worked with soldiers returning home until the conclusion of her service in 1972. Evans completed a total of six years in the Army Nurse Corps.

We saw the results of war every day in every patient—twelve, fourteen hours, whatever the length of our shift happened to be that day. Each one had a unique story to tell about Vietnam. How many patients did we treat? Thousands.

One night in Vietnam that I can't forget was the night the Sappers tried to get in through the concertina wire. Sappers were enemy personnel tasked with breaching our defenses. They were lightly clothed and adept at threading through our defenses. Their main objective was delivering high-explosive satchel charges to inflict maximum damage to our most vital interior positions.

That night, one of our guards was shot out of the tower. Our patients were coming to us by chopper within twenty minutes, and that night, a chopper came in and it was shaking the hooch where we lived. And I thought, what is that? Well, it was a Chinook helicopter. The Chinooks were these huge, heavy-lift double-rotor helicopters that could carry close to 7,000 pounds. They brought a Chinook in, heavily loaded with patients.

Now, all these new patients are starting to come in, but they're not wounded, they're sick. Why are these guys so sick? They were dehydrated, they were dirty, and there was vomit everywhere. There was no lighting. We worked in the dark at Pleiku because our hospital could not be lit because we got hit too often with rockets and mortars, so we had to use our flashlights.

I told my medic to just hold the flashlight until I could get the IV started. And then we went to the next, and the next, and the next. They were out there, stranded. And to my first patient, I said, "Well, you're safe now. You're going to live." He was so dehydrated that I could hardly find his vein because it collapsed, and he was dirty. So the scrubbing and cleaning were necessary, and then, just by feel, I was able to start his IV.

And then we went to the next, and the next, and the next. I was one lone nurse working with one lone medic. These patients all needed lifesaving care, and we were all they got. It was our job to do whatever it took under whatever circumstances to save their life. There were twenty-eight patients that night that we started with IVs and got some life going back into them. All those men survived.

You didn't come first. Your patients came first. That was just part of why we were there. Was I afraid of dying? I think by that time, I was so numb. I had resigned myself to it. Well, if I die here, that's my lot. Just like the men, I resigned myself to accept whatever happens, and I might not come home. Just when we got good at what we were doing in Vietnam, we left. Same with the guys, the infantrymen, the soldiers; once they were experienced, they were sent home.

When I knew I was going home, I learned from all the reports that it was going to be hostile for us. I'm hearing they're protesting the soldiers because this is coming from soldiers who have rotated out, gone home, and then decided to come back. They're telling us how when they went home, they got spit on.

That era is just beyond me. How could our society have turned its back on our own soldiers? How could they not separate the war from the warrior?

I am proud of my generation. We stepped up and served, and we were as honorable as the greatest generation. And my soldiers, my patients, were just as brave as World War II veterans.

These young men are suffering and dying in Vietnam, and yet they're coming home to a country that is not supporting them but denigrating them. I never thought about how we'd be treated because who would spit on a nurse? Nurses save lives, right? Well, I found out that their animosity was also directed at us.

I'm now back home at a civilian hospital in San Antonio, Texas, and I think I'm doing fine with Vietnam. It's in my memories. It's just in the recess of my mind and I'm not thinking about Vietnam, or at least I thought I wasn't. One night, an operating room nurse comes over to me and says I'm needed in the OR immediately for an emergency. And I said I am not an operating room nurse.

She insisted that I go because they needed help in the operating room. So, I scrubbed in, and there was a small child on the operating room table, and the child was hemorrhaging, and the surgeon was throwing bloody sponges into the basin for me to count.

When this happened, I had no idea what a flashback was. I smelled the blood. I saw the blood. I was immersed in a situation that I didn't know anything about. So now I'm out of control.

I was an excellent nurse when I was in my environment where I had skills; my skill sets were honed from serving in Vietnam, and I was good in the intensive care unit and in the recovery room. Now I'm in the operating room, and I'm standing there, and all of a sudden I freeze: I'm right back in Vietnam.

Viscerally and mentally, I'm in Vietnam. And it was so shocking to me. And I stood there frozen, and I wasn't functioning. The surgeon is now swearing at me and the operating room nurse is acting like she can't believe that I'm behaving in such a manner.

What kind of nurse would just stand there and do nothing? And after I left and went into the recovery room, I never received that patient because that little patient died on the operating room table. I went home and I started to shake. It was an evening shift, and I think I shook all night and couldn't sleep. The next day, I went to human resources and resigned.

I had gone from being a nurse who felt very skilled and was very competent to feeling that I was incompetent and couldn't do my job.

But it wasn't until after I attended the wall and the dedication that I couldn't keep those memories away anymore. They just came, and it seems like I never had a wake and I never had a funeral for all those men and women who died in Vietnam.

Now, I was just beginning to grieve after all these years. The grieving process was beginning. So, one by one, faces would come back, names would come back, and I was grieving for each one of them. Then I learned of the controversy about the wall itself, and the people who were building it were being criticized because it was black and beneath the ground. They had all kinds of reasons.

They didn't like the design, and they didn't like the designer, Maya Lynn, because she happened to be Asian.

So, a compromise was struck and a figurative sculpture would be added which would satisfy the opposition. The opposition meant men, mostly Vietnam veterans and some others who supported the wall of the Vietnam Veterans Memorial concept.

But they didn't like Maya Lin's concept. So they commissioned Frederick Hart, a sculptor, and told him to design a statue of three men. I soon saw a picture of this in the paper and realized they had forgotten someone—the women.

People would go to the memorial and see the sculpture of men, and they would think only men served in Vietnam. To me, they had overlooked one of the most important contingents of the Vietnam War and that was the women who were there to save the lives of the men. It was around 1983, and I told my husband that there was something I needed to do. If they're going to add a statue for the men, we need to have one for the women.

I officially founded the Vietnam Women's Memorial effort in the spring of 1984. Now, years later, we're at the final hearing, and the vote to approve it has to be unanimous.

I had written a long speech that I was going to give, and as I went up to the podium and stood before the hearing, before the committee members, I realized I only needed to say one thing, and I didn't need to read it. I said, "Is not honoring the women who served during the Vietnam era of preeminent and lasting historical significance." I sat down, and the place went quiet. They took the vote, and it was unanimous, and that was the final.

— Diane Carlson Evans

★★★

Sculptor Glenna Goodacre submitted a design that received honorable mention and was selected as the statue. The Goodacre statue now stands on the National Mall in Washington, DC. The bronze sculpture is 7'0" tall and features four figures: three women and a wounded soldier.

The Vietnam Women's Memorial was dedicated before a crowd of thousands on November 11, 1993.

To learn more about Diane Carlson Evans please check out her book, *Healing Wounds.*

Source:

Diane Carlson interview with the American Legion September 20, 2017

"About the Author Amazon Books Diane Carlson"

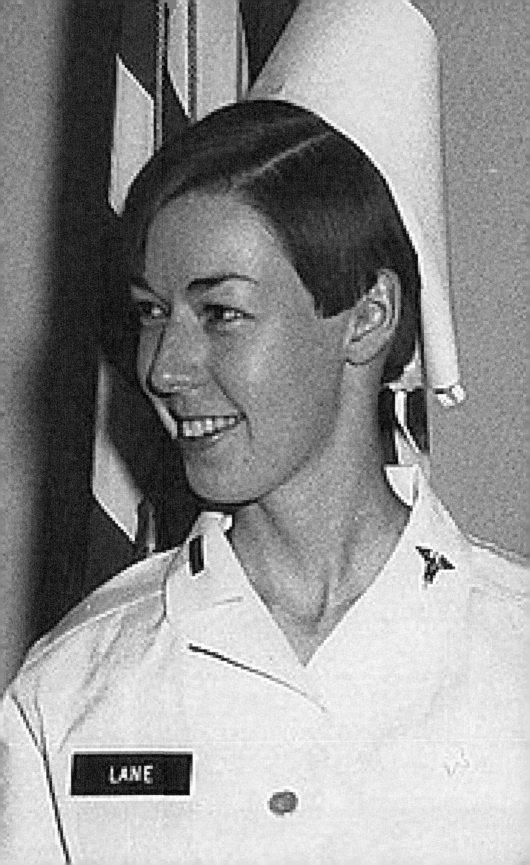

Sharon Lane

Approximately 11,000 American women were stationed in Vietnam during the War. Eight servicewomen—who were all nurses—died during the war. Among these, twenty-five-year-old Sharon Lane was the only one killed by hostile fire.

Born and raised in Zanesville, Ohio, Lane always believed she would someday become a nurse. She was accepted into the Aultman Hospital School of Nursing in Ohio and joined the Army Nurse Corps on April 18, 1968.

Lane received her orders one year later and was deployed to Vietnam as a lieutenant with the 312th Evacuation Hospital. Like most new nurses, on her arrival, Lane was given the unpopular assignment of nursing in the Vietnamese Ward, where many of the civilians had diseases that compounded any war wounds. That ward was not on the sewer system, and many Vietnamese didn't know how to use the "honey buckets" provided for human waste, so to add to the misery, that area of the camp always reeked of bodily waste.

After a few weeks, Lane was scheduled to be transferred from the Vietnamese Ward to one treating American soldiers, but she chose to remain there to take care of sick and wounded children. Because the area around the 312th Evacuation Hospital was often targeted by enemy rockets, the nurses learned to quickly grab their flak vests, helmets, and bunker bags and dive into the safety of the bunkers when incoming rounds started coming in.

On the morning of June 8, 1969, the 312th Evacuation Hospital was struck by a salvo of enemy rocket fire. As the sounds of the first incoming rockets were reported throughout the hospital, Lieutenant Lane, thinking only of the welfare of her patients, rushed to her ward to protect her wounded men from further harm.

At this time, the ward took a direct hit from an enemy rocket. The explosion produced metal fragments that struck Lieutenant Lane, taking her life. Lane died instantly when the fragment struck her neck. She was one month shy of her twenty-sixth birthday. Another twenty-seven servicemen and women were wounded that day, and a Vietnamese child was also killed in the blast.

"We were all just relaxing before waking the patients up at six A.M. I was sitting behind the desk and Lieutenant Lane was sitting on an empty bed when that rocket hit," said US Army Nurse Lt. Patricia Carr.

On June 4th, four days before her death, Lane wrote a positive, upbeat letter to her parents about how quiet it was. She also described the intense heat and humidity and the soldiers in her care. She added that her unit had just reached a milestone by treating its ten-thousandth patient since arriving in Vietnam the previous September.

A portion of that letter reads as follows:

Start "nights" tomorrow, so don't have to get up early tomorrow, which is a nice thought. It's still very quiet around here. Haven't gotten mortared for a couple of weeks now. See you sooner.

On June 14, 1969, US Army Lieutenant Sharon Lane was finally laid to rest in a full military honors funeral at the Lane at Sunset Hills Burial Park in Canton, Ohio. Lane was also the recipient of the Bronze Star with Valor.

Those who served with Lt. Lane said the following:

I was in Chu Lai when that 122mm rocket randomly took the life of one of our best. I was one of the officers that briefed Lt. Lane when she arrived in country. I routinely think of her. It was a very sad day for everyone. Was not supposed to happen.
—**Don Egan**

I was the Military Police Desk Sergeant on that Sunday morning, June 8, 1969, when we took incoming rockets into Chu Lai from the mountains several miles away. One hit the 312th Evac Hospital, and killed Lt. Lane and wounded one of the MPs there guarding the Ward. I hit the Siren Alarm that was activated when there was incoming fire at Chu Lai.

It was a very short time later that we learned of her death. In 2001, her mother attended the Americal Division Reunion in Ohio, and many visited her grave. She is always remembered, never forgotten, and beloved by fellow veterans for her service and sacrifice. RIP. —**Sgt. Wes Haun**

When the blast happened, I was close, so I went looking for you. It was too late... There was nothing I could do. You were a kind, gentle soul, and I'm sorry you didn't stay in the I.C.U. with us, but it was not meant to be. You seemed at peace. God Bless You. —**Don Rich**

I was the Supply Sergeant at the 312th Evac., when Sharon was killed. Because there were a couple of medical personnel in my hooch that worked on Ward Four, I had met Sharon. The night before she died, I was sitting in front of my hooch when Sharon walked by on her way to work. We called to her and she came over. We were drinking beer. I asked if she wanted a beer. She said she would take half a glass.

When the rocket hit, we went to the bunker out back. Then someone said it hit Ward Four. We ran up there, but... well, there was a gaping hole in the hallway between Ward Four 'A' and Ward Four 'B'. I guess I also inventoried her belongings. I went to her services. We all cried. I cry every time I go to The Wall and see her name there. Not long known, but long remembered! God Bless You, Missy!
—Gary Del Carlo

A list of the other women heroes who died in Vietnam:

- 2nd Lieutenant Carol Ann Drazba and 2nd Lieutenant Elizabeth Ann Jones were both killed on February 18, 1966, in a non-combat helicopter crash.

- 1st Lieutenant Hedwig Diane Orlowski and Captain Eleanor Grace Alexander were both killed on November 30, 1967, also in a non-combat plane crash.

- 2nd Lieutenant Pamela Dorothy Donovan died on July 8, 1968, a victim of suicide after less than three months in-country.

- Lieutenant Colonel Annie Ruth Graham died on August 14, 1968, of a stroke.

- Captain Mary Therese Klinker was killed on April 9, 1975, in a non-combat plane crash while trying to evacuate Vietnamese orphans.

Source:

Women in Vietnam: Sharon Ann Lane - National Veterans Memorial and Museum. https://nationalvmm.org/women-in-vietnam-sharon-ann-lane/

First Lieutenant Sharon Ann Lane - The Army Historical Foundation. https://armyhistory.org/first-lieutenant-sharon-ann-lane/

(1970). The BG News May 26, 1970. https://core.ac.uk/download/234744716.pdf

Mary Therese Klinker

Twelve minutes after takeoff, an explosion rocked the plane as the lower rear fuselage was torn apart. The locks in the loading ramp of the C-5 military transport plane had just failed. The explosive decompression rocked the interior, hurling passengers and equipment throughout the aircraft. To add to the terror, the interior was instantly filled with smoke and fog.

The pilots frantically worked the controls, but almost all maneuverability was lost. Control and trim cables to the rudder and elevators were shredded, leaving only one aileron and wing spoilers operating. The pilots wrestled at the controls, regaining some control using engine thrust. The pilots managed to turn the crippled smoking plane and began to descend in an attempt to pull off an emergency landing.

★★★

Mary Klinker was born in Lafayette, Indiana, and studied nursing at St. Elizabeth's School of Nursing. In January of 1970, Klinker joined the US Air Force, became a flight nurse, and was promoted to captain. After being assigned to the 10th Aeromedical Evacuation Squadron, she was temporarily assigned to Clark Air Base in the Philippines.

As the end of the Vietnam War approached, a mission called Operation Baby Lift began with the goal of evacuating over two thousand orphans from Saigon.

By April 3, 1975, the city of Da Nang had fallen and the North Vietnamese Army continued its march forward. With Saigon under attack and about to fall, President Gerald Ford announced that the US government would begin airlifting orphans in a series of flights.

When US businessman Robert Macauley learned that evacuating the surviving orphans would take more than a week due to the lack of transport planes, he chartered a Boeing 747 and arranged for three hundred orphans to leave the country. Cash-strapped at the time, Macauley paid for the trip by mortgaging his house.

Flights continued until attacks by the North Vietnamese Army and Viet Cong on Tan Son Nhut Air Base rendered any flights further impossible. By the final flight, approximately 3,300 infants and children had been airlifted. Along with Operation New Life, over 110,000 refugees were evacuated from Vietnam. Over 2,500 orphans were relocated and adopted into families in the United States and its allies, but the mission was not without a heart-wrenching tragedy.

On April 3, 1975, at 4:03 PM, the first transport flight of Operation Baby Lift took off from Tan Son Nhut Airbase outside of Saigon. Captain Mary Klinker was one of the flight nurses assigned to care for the orphans as they were transported.

The Air Force C-5A Galaxy military transport aircraft was bound for Clark Air Base in the Philippines. Captain Dennis Traynor was the aircraft commander, and Captain Tilford Harp was the co-pilot. Twelve minutes after takeoff, when the aircraft had passed through 23,000 feet, the rear loading ramp's locks suddenly failed. This caused an explosive decompression and massive structural damage to the plane.

Control cables were severed, leaving only one wing spoiler and aileron working. In addition to their problems, two hydraulic systems catastrophically failed, causing more flight control problems. Traynor and Harp regained marginal control of the aircraft using engine power thrust. They turned back toward Tan Son Nhut for an emergency landing.

As the C-5 passed 4,000 feet and was turning to the final approach, it quickly became apparent that they could not reach the runway. Traynor applied full power to hold the nose up while Harp fought the controls to maintain a wings-level attitude.

Just off the ground, Traynor reduced power to idle and the C-5 touched down in a rice paddy. It skidded about 1,000 feet before becoming airborne again, violently striking a tall dike and breaking into four parts.

The cargo compartment was destroyed, killing 141 of the 149 orphans and attendants. Only three of the 152 in the troop compartment were killed.

Five of the flight crew, three of the medical team, and three other servicemen lost their lives; of the original 328 passengers aboard, 175 survived.

Captain Mary Klinker was only twenty-seven years old when she was killed. She was the last nurse and the only member of the US Air Force Nurse Corps to be killed during the Vietnam War. Captain Klinker was posthumously awarded the Airman's Medal for Heroism and the Meritorious Service Medal.

Almost fifty years later, US Army Medic Lonnie Wiseman, who volunteered to help during Operation Baby Lift, stated in a CGTN America interview, "It was my way of giving back and to honor the sacrifice of the fifty-eight thousand US soldiers that were lost." Survivors tell their story:

Chris Norland

My name is Chris Norland, and I survived a plane crash as a baby. I was born at the end of the Vietnam War. I don't have a birthday, so I don't really know exactly when I was born. I was put on the first plane out. It was a C-5 Galaxy, which, at the time it, was the largest airplane in the world.

Because I was a baby, they put me in a shoebox, and they put that on the airplane. After a few minutes in the air, there was a malfunction on the plane and the rear cargo doors blew. Because I was young, I was in the upper half of the plane, and therefore I survived.

After we lost power, the pilots tried to regain control, and so they ended up speeding up the plane and they turned around and crashed into a rice field. The plane skidded for about a quarter of a mile and then skipped up back in the air and then crashed into a dike. We were full of fuel and the plane exploded into four parts and everything caught on fire.

The plane was about a mile from the road, so the Americans had to walk really far across the rice field and the helicopters arrived, but they couldn't land, and so they would hover above us. There was this smoke and fire everywhere, but they would lower one rescue worker at a time, rescue one person, and bring it back up in a basket.

But because the rescue operation was slow, some people actually survived the crash, but either burned to death or drowned in the mud. Those of us who survived the crash were sent to the United States.

When I arrived in the USA, I didn't have any paperwork, so it was actually really difficult to prove that I existed. All I had was my little three-by-five card that said I was from Sancta Maria Orphanage. After living seven years in the USA, I was eligible to apply for US citizenship.

I went down to the courthouse, and I swore to be an American. Like all the other immigrants, and I had to miss a day of school. The next day at school, my teacher said, "What did you do?" And I said, "I became an American," and I remember really clearly this little girl walks to the front of the room and reads me a welcome to America speech and every kid in my grade made me Welcome to America cards. This is what

America means to me. After the tragic events of September 11, 2001, I joined the United States Navy to be a pilot. — *October 2020 Buzzfeed interview*

David Leduc

I'm living the American dream, having a big family, a good career, and owning a few small businesses. Life is good! — 2015 interview with Maria Caccomo

Thuay Williams

My name is Thuay Williams, and I was one of the orphans brought to the United States. I was five years old when my mother put me on the C-5 cargo plane. As a mixed-race child of a US soldier, my mother knew the North Vietnamese would consider me the enemy.

She didn't know that the plane was overfilled, and I was later removed from it and put on another plane the next day. She was told that I died on the original April 3rd flight. After being adopted in the US, I remember for the first time not being hungry, dirty, or wet.

Because of the great people, the heroes who stepped out to save the lives of children like me, I have had the opportunity to accomplish much in life. As a high schooler, I played in the Junior World Soccer Cup, and I proudly served the country I love in the US Army as a tank mechanic.

I've organized over thirty humanitarian missions to help impoverished countries around the world, and I now coach high school track and soccer. I do not think I would have survived as a five-year-old in Vietnam. I owe everything to all those who were part of Operation Baby Lift. —2022 Pan Am Museum interview

The other military personnel who died due to the crash were Lieutenant Colonel William Willis, Captain Edgar Melton, Master Sgt. Joe Castro, Master Sgt. Denning Johnson, Master Sgt. Wendle Payne, Technical Sgt. Felizardo Aguillon, Technical Sgt. William M. Parker, Staff Sgt. Donald Dionne, Staff Sgt. Kenneth Nance and Staff Sgt. Michael Paget.

Source:

Viet Nam – Operation Babylift – America On Coffee | The Rush Hour Blog. https://therushhour.net/2021/04/14/timber-break/

Mary T. Klinker - Mary T Klinker Veterans Resource Center. https://www.mtkvets.org/our-mission/mary-t-klinker/

May | 2008 | Nuke's. https://nukegingrich.wordpress.com/2008/05/

The enemy of my enemy - The Australian National University. https://researchportalplus.anu.edu.au/en/publications/the-enemy-of-my-enemy

"Courage is grace under pressure,"

— Ernest Hemingway

Sarah Blum

"There was no time for emotions. I could not show my emotions, or the soldiers who came in wounded would have thought it meant they were going to die. Initially, I had gut-wrenching emotional reactions of horror and incredible sadness at the utter destruction of these beautiful young soldiers. I saw the worst of humanity and what War does to hearts, minds, and bodies. There were so many young men with irreparably mutilated and mangled bodies. The constant flow of mass casualties left no time or energy to allow my feelings to flow. I had to shut them down."

— *US Army Nurse Sarah Blum*

Clink, clink, clink... the sound of dozens of pieces of shrapnel being dropped into their metal basin trays echoed around the operating room. Doctors and nurses worked feverishly extracting the foreign metal invaders wreaking havoc in the bodies of young US Soldiers. Constant enemy mortar attacks, monsoons flooding the operating rooms, and swarms of giant red locusts affectionately known as 'Nurse Killers' were only a fraction of the challenges Army nurse Sarah Blum would endure at the 12th Evacuation Hospital in Vietnam.

Sarah L. Blum was born in Atlantic City, New Jersey, on December 5, 1939. Before joining the Army, she was a nurse in the intensive care unit at a Los Angeles hospital. Sarah's father served in the signal corps during World War II, and her brother was a crew chief on Army helicopters during the Cold War. Sarah joined the US Army in March 1966 and was commissioned as a first lieutenant.

Sarah received her orders to Vietnam in January 1967, landing at the chaotic Bien Hoa airbase. Before getting her bearings, she was whisked onto a bus fitted with armor and driven to the 90th Replacement Battalion. After a whirlwind three-day course on everything an American in Vietnam should know, she was ordered to the 67th Evacuation Hospital. However, fate stepped in, and she volunteered to go to the 12th Evacuation Hospital in Cu Chi.

The 12th Evacuation Hospital was on the edge of the Iron Triangle, where the heaviest fighting took place in 1967. The 12th Hospital was the largest user of fresh blood in all of Vietnam. It also supported the 5th Infantry Battalion, the First Infantry, and the 82nd and 101st Airborne. The enemy also noted its importance and was constantly under mortar attacks.

★★★

The night before I left the 90th Battalion to head to the 12th Evacuation Hospital, I ran into my old drill Sergeant from basic training, and he asked me where I would be sent. His face drained of color when I told him, and he said, "Get it changed. You don't want to go there! That is the worst place to be; it is where all the fighting is, and it is not safe." I told him I couldn't change it now because earlier that week, I switched with a young nurse who had the same MOS (Military Occupational Specialty).

That young nurse was scared and crying because she did not want to go to the 12th Evacuation Hospital. I was initially assigned to the 67th Evacuation Hospital at Qui Nhon and offered to switch with her. I first wanted to help the young woman but also to be where the action was. The chief nurse agreed because of the severe emotional distress of the other young nurse. My thoughts at the time were that I didn't care where I was stationed as long as I could help our soldiers. My old drill Sergeant was not happy about it and told me to keep my head down and stay safe.

My footlocker and duffle bag were taken by truck, and I was put on a Huey helicopter to go to the 12th Evacuation Hospital. My first helicopter ride was scary because they did not have doors. I felt very vulnerable sitting in a canvas seat in the wide-open space while flying in a War zone, and if you think that was frightening, the landing was worse.

When they arrived at the hospital, the helicopter crew would not land the helicopter. They told me I had to jump out onto the helipad. The helicopter was very loud, and it was hard to hear over the rotor blades' sounds. I kept pointing down with my arm and finger, "Put this thing down," they kept shaking their heads and saying, "Jump." They hovered the helicopter about six feet over the helipad, so I had no choice but to jump. I guess that was my initiation. Or was it?

Next, I saluted our very stiff executive officer, who was trying to find out where I belonged. He looked starched and professional and asked me, 'What is that?' pointing to my ukulele case. I brought a baritone ukulele with me so that I had an instrument to play while there. My answer was a joke to lighten up the situation, "It is a machine gun; I thought I might need it over here." That was the wrong thing to say to him, and for the next twenty minutes, he yelled at me for being disrespectful and finally told me where to report."

We had two Quonset huts for our operating rooms. The main one was called Arizona, and in it, we had five different partitioned areas that counted as a room. Each area had an operating room, which included a table, equipment for anesthesia, a stainless steel table I would use for instruments and sterile supplies, and an over-the-table stand that we used to hold suture material and extra instruments.

We had one shift only, from nine AM until we were done with scheduled cases for the day and then all the new cases generated by the War. We often worked around the clock, but the average was about sixteen hours daily. I was on call four nights a week.

We had soldiers with wounds all over their bodies or only parts of their bodies left intact. Often, they lost arms, legs, and eyes, or they had shrapnel that tore through major organs in their bodies, which we had to repair. I saw the worst of War and what it does to the land and the human beings on it. We were constantly targets for the enemy and mortared often. Fortunately, I was never hit, and the worst attack the hospital received happened a month after I left.

During my first mortar attack at the 12th Evacuation Hospital, I was actually taking a shower. A young soldier told me I needed to immediately get to the bunker. Covered in soap, I tried to protest, but he threatened to carry me there if I didn't immediately go, which I did. Later, during the attack, while I was sitting in the bunker covered in soap and wearing only a robe, I was ordered into the Operating Room. Numerous casualties were coming in due to the onslaught of the mortar attack. I remember running through the mortars in a zig-zag pattern, and somehow, I made it into the OR in one piece.

Many crazy things happened over there. We had these giant flying locusts we called Nurse Killers. They were huge red locusts that not only hopped but could also fly, and they would infest the 12th in enormous swarms. One night, after an exhausting day of surgery, I finally made it back to my cot at around three AM. I collapsed forward into my cot only to have one of those giant locusts land on the middle of my back. I couldn't reach it and screamed and yelled until another nurse pulled it off my back. We did get our revenge, though, and we kept our own body count of those disgusting red bugs. If we killed one, we would stick their bodies onto this big corkboard using a 21 gauge syringe tip. It sounds crazy, but with the stress we dealt with, you needed to find things to blow off some of the steam.

After I had been there for about six months, I had a major emotional experience. A young red-headed soldier was hit by American artillery and had the lower half of his body blasted severely. From his hip bones down, he was black, charred, and bleeding. We had four surgeons look at him to decide what they could save and what they could do for him.

I was standing in his blood for hours as we worked on him and what was left. In the end, some large skin flaps were covering the remainder of his pelvis. He was literally half a man. I was okay during the surgery because I learned to be numb to it all, but then, on day three, the day he came into the OR for the closure of his skin flaps, I snapped.

He was at one end of the Quonset hut on a stretcher, and I came in from the opposite end. As I walked toward him, I saw the flat sheet covering the stretcher, and half the length of it was flat because there was nothing there. Finally, my eyes saw the bump that was his bandaged hips and then his torso covered with the sheet, and finally his face and eyes. My eyes followed all that up to his face, and when I saw his red hair and blue eyes, something inside me snapped, and I ran out the doors.

Some assault helicopters were flying overhead at that moment, and I shouted as loudly as I could through my rage and tears at the choppers, "Kill, Kill, Kill—that is all you know how to do! I hate this War, I hate this War!" I have no memory of what I did or how long I was going around the Hospital yelling at the sky, but I ended up in front of my chief nurse, telling her, "You have got to get me out of the OR. I can't take it anymore. Put me on the malaria ward or something." She shook her head and said, I cannot do that; you just need a rest. Take a few days and go down to the beach at Vung Tau and get yourself together."

I left Vietnam, at the same place where I came in at the Bien Hoa airbase. A couple hundred of us lined up on the tarmac in the 110° heat, waiting for what we called the 'freedom bird,' the plane that would take us home. We all felt like sitting ducks because the airbase was constantly being hit with mortars. The enemy seemed to ramp up their attacks when they knew our soldiers were waiting to go home. I was terrified that I had lived through that year of hell and would be killed as I was waiting to leave.

I know I was not the only one who thought and felt that. When the plane arrived, it was pink and orange, Southwest Airlines color. Everyone was tense until the moment the plane actually lifted off the tarmac. At that point, I could hear everyone taking in a much-needed, deep breath. It was a collective loud intake of air and relief that we made it out alive.

When I arrived at Travis Air Force Base in San Francisco, they would not let us off the plane for two hours and told us not to wear our uniforms. It was not what I expected. It was very disappointing, but I was numb.

I was heading for Los Angeles to see my nurse friends I worked with before going to Vietnam. It was late at night, and I was so glad to have someone happy to see me finally. The next day, I had my first experience of culture shock. When I was on the way to the Hospital to visit my friend, an ambulance came by with the siren blaring. I instinctively dove into the foot-well of the car as though expecting an attack. My friend, Ellie, was shocked by my reaction, and so was I. Later, we went into a supermarket, and when I stepped onto the pad in front of the door, and the door suddenly flew open, I jumped back. It took me a while to acclimate back into society.

I stopped telling anyone that I was a nurse who served in Vietnam. In 1970, I married another Vietnam Veteran, and we had two children. In 1981, my PTSD suddenly came back in a flash. I was driving to work, and the song "Tie a Yellow Ribbon Around the Old Oak Tree" started playing. It was dedicated to the US hostages coming home from Iran, and all of these emotions started pouring out of me. What did they do to deserve a welcome home? What about us? The thing I say about the War and PTSD is it's the gift that keeps on giving. Here I was, thirteen years later, since Vietnam, and it was still inside me.

74

I was part of the very first women veterans group at the Seattle Vet Center for sixteen weeks and then did another sixteen weeks after that to deal with my PTSD symptoms. That was not enough, and by 1984, I was doing therapy with a trauma specialist until 1987. From then on, I have worked with veterans and civilians to help them heal their PTSD. Today, I became a black belt in Aikido, learned to play the drums, and finished writing my second book on PTSD and healing.

My final thoughts about the War are the good memories of my experience, mainly the esprit de corps we had together at our Hospital, saving many lives, and loving my brother and sister service members.

War is never okay. War destroys life in all forms. We must separate the War from the warrior and welcome home our soldiers who go in our name, even if we do not agree with why they were sent. I feel proud of my service now, but for many years, I did not.

— *Sarah L. Blum*

Sarah Blum was the recipient of the Army Commendation Medal and was awarded the Certificate of Achievement for exemplary service at Madigan Army Hospital in 1968. To learn more about this incredible Vietnam Veteran and hero, please check out her books: "Warrior Nurse: PTSD and Healing" and "Women Under Fire."

Source:
https://vva.org/books-in-review/women-under-fire-by-sarah-l-blum/
https://www.veteranrites.org/blog/2020/4/22/your-magnificence-vietnam-vet-sarah-blum
https://cherrieswriter.com/2024/10/12/a-vietnam-war-nurse/

Women Warriors
throughout History

Mary Edwards Walker

A surgeon, an abolitionist, and a spy.

Throughout US history, there have been 3,536 Medal of Honor recipients. However, only one was a woman, and her medal was rescinded just before she died.

Mary Walker was born on November 26, 1832, in the town of Oswego, New York. She was the last of five daughters of abolitionists Alvah and Vesta Walker. Her parents always stressed education and encouraged all their children to think freely. They also allowed all their daughters to wear the "bloomer" style pants instead of the corsets and skirts women were required to wear at the time.

Mary's parents started the first free school in Oswego so their daughters would be just as educated as any other child—boy or girl. Outside of school, all the Walker children helped by working on the family farm.

After attending seminary school, Walker became a teacher, but she knew she had always wanted to become a doctor. She worked as a teacher until she saved enough money for medical school. Walker was accepted into Syracuse Medical College and received her medical degree in 1855. Walker became the only other woman to graduate from Syracuse after Elizabeth Blackwell.

When the Civil War broke out in 1861, Walker set out to join the Union's efforts. She went to Washington but was not allowed to serve as a medical officer because she was a female. She decided to remain an unpaid volunteer surgeon at the US Patent Office Hospital in Washington.

At the time, the US Army had no female surgeons, so Walker was only allowed to work as a nurse in the temporary hospitals erected around the capital. In 1862, Walker was sent to Virginia, where she started treating wounded soldiers near the front lines at Chattanooga and Fredericksburg.

In 1863, her petition to practice as a surgeon was finally accepted. She became the first female US Army surgeon as a "Contract Acting Assistant Surgeon (civilian)" by the Army of the Cumberland.

Despite protests from her superiors, Walker routinely crossed battle lines to care for soldiers and civilians. In April of 1864, Walker was taken prisoner by Confederate troops and suspected of being a spy. She was held as a prisoner of war for four months at the dangerous Castle Thunder prison near Richmond, the Confederate capital.

While imprisoned, she refused to accept the women's clothes her captors provided. She would wear men's clothes her entire life because, she said, "Men's styled clothing is not only more comfortable but also more hygienic. It also makes working as a surgeon in hospitals easier because it frees my movement." Walker later claimed to have even worn pants under her skirt at her wedding.

Walker was finally released from prison in August of 1864 as part of a prisoner exchange with other medical doctors. In September 1864, she was contracted as the assistant surgeon of the Ohio 52nd Infantry. During the remainder of the Civil War, Walker served at the Louisville Women's Prison Hospital and an orphan asylum in Tennessee.

At the end of the Civil War in 1865, President Andrew Johnson awarded Walker the Medal of Honor for Meritorious Service. However, she never received a military pension because she had never been officially commissioned in the army. A few years later, in 1871, Walker wrote and published an autobiographical book titled *Essays on Women's Rights*.

After her work during the Civil War, she became an outspoken advocate for women's rights. She famously wore pants and consistently advocated for "dress reform." In 1870, she was arrested by local police in New Orleans because she was dressed in the same manner as a man.

This was not her only arrest for wearing men's clothes, which included her signature top hat. Walker responded to criticism of her sartorial choices by saying, "I don't wear men's clothes; I wear my own style of clothes that I choose."

She also fought for suffrage and tried to register to vote in 1871 but was denied. She believed the US Constitution already granted women the right to vote. In 1912 and 1914, she testified in front of the US House of Representatives to support women's suffrage.

As suffragists moved towards advocating for a federal amendment and Walker was ostracized by more mainstream suffragists for her choice to wear pants, jackets, and top hats, she became increasingly distanced from the movement. Later in life, Walker opened up her home to others who were harassed or arrested for not conforming to traditional ideas of how people should dress.

In 1916, the US government started a program to review the eligibility of all Medal of Honor recipients. Later that year, Walker was stripped of the medal and her name removed from all military documents. This did not prevent Walker from openly wearing her Medal of Honor award until her death at the ripe old age of eighty-six.

Mary Edwards Walker died of illness on February 21, 1919. She left her final instructions in her will to be buried in a plain black suit.

President Jimmy Carter, in 1977, formerly restored the Medal of Honor to Mary Walker's name.

Source:

Biography: Mary Edwards Walker

https: //www.womenshistory.org/education-resources/biographies/mary-edwards-walker

Kerri Lee Alexander, NWHM Fellow | 2018-2019 |

"Well-behaved women
seldom make history."

– Laurel Thatcher Ulrich

Flora Sandes

The only British woman to see combat on the front lines during World War One.

It was a bitterly cold morning in November of 1916 near Bitola, Macedonia. The Royal Serbian Army was pressing forward against Bulgarian forces in brutal hand-to-hand fighting on a snowy hillside. A Bulgarian grenade landed at the feet of Sergeant Major Flora Sandes; the intense blast knocked her off her feet.

As she lay in semi-consciousness in the snow, trying to recover her wits, Sandes recalled, "I could see nothing. It was as though I had gone suddenly blind, but I felt the tail of an overcoat sweep across my face. Instinctively, I clutched it with my left hand and must have held on for two or three yards before I fainted."

Sgt. Sandes was part of nearly 30,000 Royal Serbian Army troops fighting from their base in Greece. Their mission was to fight their way over the border and back into Serbia, which had been occupied by Bulgarian forces a year earlier.

Flora Sandes is still celebrated in Serbia as a legendary war hero and her image was adorned on a Serbian stamp in 2015. What makes her story more incredible is that Sandes was not Serbian but British. Sandes was born January 22, 1876, in Yorkshire. She was the only British woman to engage in combat on the front lines in World War One.

While most women at the time were encouraged to perform domestic roles, Flora Sandes was knocking down barriers by fighting in close combat. But how did Sandes rise to the esteemed rank of senior captain while being decorated with seven medals of honor? And for the Serbia Army no less?

The answer is revealed in what Sandes telegraphed for her future self; early on in life, she expressed a desire to be a soldier and experience the life of combat.

She enjoyed shooting guns for target practice growing up and learned to drive at a relatively young age. In 1914, at the outbreak of World War One, Sandes tried becoming a nurse but was rejected due to a lack of qualifications. Refusing to be deterred, Sandes eventually joined the Saint John Ambulance Brigade, which was founded by American nurse Mabel Grouitch.

On August 12, 1914, Sandes departed for Serbia with a group of thirty-six women to try to aid the humanitarian crisis. In her autobiography, "An English Woman-Sergeant in the Serbian Army," which was based on her writing from letters and diaries, Sandes recounts her harrowing journey, traveling to Serbia as a volunteer nurse. She worked there as a nurse for eighteen months before becoming a soldier.

During the typhus epidemic, she volunteered to go to Valjevo, which was at the epicenter of the disease and where several Serbian doctors and many nurses had already died from the illness. The same fate very nearly overtook her, but fortunately, she recovered.

However, she soon found herself drawn deeper into the military conflict as the Serbian Army struggled against overwhelming odds. One of the most inhumane and demoralizing experiences Sandes describes in her book—the proceeds of which helped her raise funds for the Serbian Army—took place during the Serbian Army's retreat across Albania in late 1915, known as the "Great Retreat."

The conditions were punishing: soldiers were forced to march across freezing mountains with scant supplies, suffering from hunger, exhaustion, and disease. Sandes vividly recounts how many of her comrades died horrifically from frostbite and or dysentery. Others were ambushed or captured by hostile local tribes.

Despite it all, Sandes took unusual comfort in the excitement of battle and fighting alongside in comradeship with her fellow soldiers. That feeling of purpose superseded any pain, suffering, or near-death experiences she had.

In her autobiography, she wrote: "Blazing hot days followed by freezing cold nights, when we lay on the bare mountainside in clothes soaked in perspiration with no covering but our overcoats; incessant fighting, weariness indescribable, but hand-in-hand with romance, adventure, and comradeship, which more than made up for everything."

Still, the cruelties of battle and the unrelenting threat of death tested Sandes' mettle. She slept in trenches during snowy nights and endured the physical and emotional toll of combat without proper equipment. Her account also describes tending to wounded comrades on the battlefield with limited medical supplies, often seeing friends die in her arms.

In 1916, during the Serbian advance on Bitola, Sandes was terribly wounded by a grenade blast. She spoke only to her closest comrades about the excruciating pain of the injury she endured. She further spoke to them of her frustrations of continuing to function as a soldier in a war-torn environment where proper medical care was often unavailable.

It took Sandes six months to recover sufficiently from her injuries before returning to the front line. By the war's end, Sandes would be awarded Serbia's highest military honor, the Order of the Karadjordje Star. She was then promoted to sergeant major in a small ceremony.

Sandes returned to England later in life to spend her last years in Suffolk. This hero passed away on November 24, 1956. A memorial plaque in Marlesford's Saint Andrews Church is dedicated to her. Sandes'personal account serves as a testament to the indomitable spirit of a rare woman who transcended the traditional roles of her time, becoming both a fighter and a symbol of courage.

Source:

The Story of Flora Sandes by David Pejčinović-Bailey MBE.
https://www.anenglishmaninthebalkans.com/p/the-story-of-flora-sandes

This Week's Top Picks in Imperial & Global History – Imperial & Global
Forum. https://imperialglobalexeter.com/2018/10/06/this-weeks-top-picks-in-imperial-global-history-222/

Captain Flora Sandes: 'the Serbian Joan of Arc'.
https://www.historyireland.com/captain-flora-sandes-the-serbian-joan-of-arc/

"The most difficult thing is the decision to act, the rest is merely tenacity."

— Amelia Earhart

Edith Cavell

"I have no fear nor shrinking. I have seen death so often that it is not strange or fearful to me ... I thank God for this ten weeks 'quiet before the end. Life has always been hurried and full of difficulty. This time of rest has been a great mercy. They have all been very kind to me here. But this I would say, standing as I do in view of God and eternity, I realize that patriotism is not enough. I must have no hatred or bitterness towards anyone."

— Edith Cavell, on the night before her execution, as recounted by Reverend Stirling Gahan, October 11, 1915.

Edith Cavell was a British nurse whose courage and compassion during World War I made her an enduring symbol of heroism.

Born December 4, 1865, in the quaint English farming village of Swardeston, Cavell was raised in a deeply religious household. She grew up watching her father's boisterous sermons at the small Anglican church where he served as the Vicar.

Poor in resources but rich in spirituality and education, her parents nurtured their four children. Cavell grew up learning about truth, dedication, the love of God, and humanity. Death was interwoven with life and never to be feared or looked away from. At the time, her parents could never have known that one day, their daughter would die with bravery and dignity for her country and be honored in the most sacred church in all of Britain, Westminister Abbey.

In 1896, Cavell worked for several months at the Fountains Fever Hospital as a nurse's assistant to see whether she could handle the rigors of nursing. Cavell's constant professionalism and attention to detail earned her acceptance into the prestigious Royal London Hospital to begin her formal training.

In 1897, the deadly Typhoid disease broke out in Kent, England, and Cavell, along with several other nurses, was sent to help those suffering.

At the outbreak of World War I in August 1914, Cavell was living in Brussels, operating a medical clinic and a nursing school. When German forces invaded Belgium, she decided to remain in the city, even though she could have easily fled back to Britain. Instead, she chose to stay and care for her patients, both soldiers and civilians, without regard to their nationality.

Her selflessness went far beyond providing medical care. Cavell secretly helped injured soldiers, both Belgian and Allied, escape German-occupied Belgium by smuggling them across the border into Holland. These daring rescue operations were dangerous, but Cavell always put others before her own safety.

In August 1915, Cavell was arrested by the German authorities. She was charged under the German Military Code with aiding the escape of enemy soldiers—a crime that carried a death sentence. Although she admitted to helping the soldiers flee, she remained steadfast in her belief that she had done the right thing. Some of those she had helped even managed to contact her to report that they had safely reached England. But the Germans were less concerned with her motives than with the fact that her actions had allowed their enemies to return to a country at war.

On the morning of May 12, 1915, Philippe Baucq, the head of the Underground, and Edith Cavell were brought north of Brussels to the Tir National Firing Range. Philippe Baucq was dragged in front of the firing squad to be shot first.

Cavell's grey eyes blazed with courage as she proudly stood before the line of eight riflemen as they slowly raised their rifles.

The physician who declared her dead found only four bullet holes in her body; four of the German soldiers could not bring themselves to fire at her and had deliberately missed. Cavell was buried where she fell, with only a small wooden cross marking her grave.

Death may have ended her life, but her murder ignited the ire of the world. The Germans soon would learn that executing Cavell would be their biggest mistake. Her killing made the front pages of newspapers all over the world. The Germans believed her death would devastate the morale of the British army and cause them to pull out of the war, but they misjudged the resolve of the British people. This heinous act created worldwide revulsion, indignation, and outrage and spurred thousands of British men to volunteer their service in the military to avenge her death.

Canadians and Australians also responded similarly. Up to this time, America had not committed to joining the war in Europe, but this barbaric murder changed the attitude of the American public. On April 6, 1917, United States soldiers joined the Allied forces to help defeat the Germans.

World War I finally ended on November 11, 1918. In May 1919, Cavell's body was disinterred and brought home to England. She was honored at Westminster Abbey and then taken to Norwich, where some of the pallbearers were the same soldiers she had helped escape the Germans.

Source:

Edith Cavell: The Other Nightingale

Detected ReferenceArthur, T. (2020). Edith Cavell: The Other Nightingale. Online Journal of Issues in Nursing, 25(2), 1-11.

Edith Cavell | National WWI Museum and Memorial

https://theworldwar.org/learn/about-wwi/edith-cavell

Detected ReferenceEdith Cavell | National WWI Museum and Memorial. https://theworldwar.org/learn/about-wwi/edith-cavell

Conversations: Guarding Our Hearts | Nurses Christian Fellowship https://ncf-jcn.org/blog/conversations-guarding-our-hearts

Detected ReferenceConversations: Guarding Our Hearts | Nurses Christian Fellowship. https://ncf-jcn.org/blog/conversations-guarding-our-hearts

"A woman is like a tea bag—you never know how strong she is until you put her in hot water."

— Eleanor Roosevelt

Jeannette Guyot

When France buckled under the pressure from German forces in WWII, many begrudgingly accepted their fates as captives to the Nazi overlords. Not Jeannette Guyot. She took up the mantle of resistance at age 22, working day and night to save all those she could, even surviving capture and months of interrogation by the Gestapo. When she finally retired at war's end, she would go down in history as one of the war's most decorated women.

It was February 8th, 1944, and Jeannette Guyot leapt from the British RAF bomber into the bitterly cold night sky above occupied France. She was not afraid — she had earned her parachute wings — but the mission she undertook was drenched in danger. She had already been captured once; if the Germans got their hands on her again, her life was over.

"I landed pretty heavily as the wind was strong, got rid of my gear and found myself in the bright moonlight," she later wrote in a letter to a superior. Suddenly, a man appeared out of the darkness. If this was an Englishman, she was well on the way to success. If this was a German, she was dead.

"All right, old chap?" he whispered to her. As he leaned in closer, he corrected himself, taken aback.

"Oh sorry, this is the first time a woman dropped on us."

Jeannette Guyot was a French resistance fighter without peer, fiercely fighting against German occupation for four long years. Even after being captured and interrogated for three months, her patriotism compelled her to return to France despite the threat of torture and execution rising with every passing day.

Guyot was born in Chalon-sur-Saône on Feb. 26, 1919, and defiance ran thick through her family's blood. When the Nazis invaded, her father Jean-Marie joined the underground force françaises combattantes (FCC). Jean-Marie paid the ultimate price for his bold opposition to the Germans; he was captured and deported to Germany in 1943, where he perished. Her mother Jeanne also participated in the FCC, and was arrested 10 days after her husband. She was sent to a concentration camp in Ravensbrück, Germany, where she would remain until the end of the war.

When her country was torn asunder by Nazi Germany, 22-year-old Jeannette did not hesitate to join the Resistance. Instead of running away or submitting to the invaders, she took advantage of her hometown's proximity to the relative safety of Vichy France to escort refugees and intelligence agents across the Saône River.

In 1941, Guyot joined the Confrérie Notre-Dame resistance network where she continued her courier work, but it wouldn't be long before disaster struck. In 1942 she was arrested by the Gestapo, and three harrowing months of interrogation followed during which a single misspoken word would've meant the end of her life. But Guyot was a determined professional, and she never broke under the extreme pressure; she left imprisonment with her cover story intact and went right back into her work with the Allies.

This all changed, however, when the resistance network was infiltrated by German intelligence. In June of 1942, Pierre Cartaud sabotaged the Resistance from the inside, leading to the arrest of many of its members and placing Guyot in mortal danger.

Betrayed and under immense threat of capture, she was forced to flee to Lyon in Vichy France. But that, too, proved to be a sinking ship. In November 1942, Germany rolled into Vichy, stomping out Resistance elements and forcing Guyot to make one of the hardest decisions of her life: She needed to immediately leave France or face her inevitable death at the hands of the Gestapo. On May 13, 1943, a British squadron discretely landed in a pasture in central France, and Guyot hastily boarded, putting her fury at the Germans into the back of her mind — for now.

Instead of succumbing to defeat, the moment she touched down in Britain she joined the French Free Forces. She worked against the Germans from London for half a year before her stubborn bravery urged her into taking a more direct approach. She underwent more intelligence training, earned her jump wings, and parachuted back into France as part of Operation Sussex. Guyot and her team would perform pivotal and immensely risky intelligence missions from behind enemy lines in the build up to the D-Day invasion.

After parachuting down into France, she made her way to Paris, where she walked into Café du Reseau with the intention to make an ally. Recruiting assets into resistance forces was a dance with the devil: Recruitment was an absolute necessity to building intelligence networks, but every new recruit came with the possibility of bringing a German plant into the ranks. In this case, Guyot's grit paid off. Madame Goubillion, owner of Café du Reseau, had her husband taken prisoner by the Germans a short time before, and was ready to go to any length to get back at the Nazi invaders.

"I remember she came into the bar," Madame Goubillon told The Observer in 1988, remembering her first encounter with Jeannette Guyot. "I knew she did this sort of work, and when she asked me, I agreed without the slightest hesitation." Even though the Gestapo had an office just down the street, Goubillon felt no fear; she had a duty to fulfill for her husband and her country.

At one point, Goubillon was hiding seven men and a cache of weapons in her tiny cellar when a German soldier marched in.

"If he had been any trouble, I would have knocked him on the head and pushed him down the well," Goubillon said, "but all he wanted was a glass of white wine and a chat about his wife and children."

The French suffered deeply for their resistance to the Nazi occupiers. Guyot's fellow Resistance operatives were routinely captured, tortured and executed for their "crimes" against the

Germans. Even worse, however, was the collective punishment perpetrated by the Nazis, in which random French civilians would be killed to punish the Resistance. By the time the war drew to a close, 30,000 French hostages had been shot to intimidate defiant members of the Resistance.

This never stopped nor even slowed the indomitable Guyot. From the moment German boots stomped into her hometown, to the Allied victory in 1945, Guyot risked her life every day to fight her clandestine war against the Nazi's who had enslaved France. She continuously set up airdrop zones and safe houses up until the Allies liberated the area.

Guyot's exceptional resolve earned her three of the Allied Powers 'top military awards: France's Croix de guerre avec palmes; America's Distinguished Service Cross; and the British George Medal. Guyot reunited with her mother after her release from a concentration camp and married one of her fellow Resistance fighters whom she'd fought side by side with.

Jeannette Guyot left the Resistance in honor, able to retire with the knowledge that she'd spent every day doing all she could to sabotage the Germans in her home country. She ended the war as one of France's most highly decorated agents, and will forever serve as a model for fearless resistance fighters standing up to the forces of fascism.

This hero passed away on April 10, 2016, at the age of 97, in eastern France. Her Awards: Legion of Honour, Distinguished Service Cross, George Medal.

Source:

The Quiet Heroine: Jeannette Guyot. https://www.historynet.com/guyot/

Obituary: Jeannette Guyot, French Resistance fighter

https://www.scotsman.com/news/obituary-jeannette-guyot-french-resistance-fighter-1477354

"Once we have a war there is only one thing to do. It must be won. For defeat brings worse things than any that can ever happen in war."

Ernest Miller Hemmingway

Virginia Hall
(losomaniku alikiri)

Virginia Hall

"Miss Hall displayed rare courage, perseverance and ingenuity; her efforts contributed materially to the successful operations of the Resistance Forces in support of the Allied Expeditionary Forces in the liberation of France."

Citation for Distinguished Service Cross awarded to Virginia Hall, 1945

President Harry Truman

Virginia Hall once wore live snakes as bracelets to school. Her mother was utterly horrified, but this was her daughter, and she would soon find out that there was nothing she could do about her: Virginia was immutable. You could say this young woman was born upright with her fists out. Her legacy would paint the picture of a woman both daring and ingenious, who would retire from the war as one of the Allies 'greatest intelligence assets.

Born in Baltimore to a well-to-do family, she would spend the rest of her life in a cold war with Barbara, her mother, who wanted her to marry a rich man and settle down with lots of money to provide her with the lifestyle she wanted. But Virginia's destiny was not that of a housewife; she had other plans and yearned for adventure. Even grievous injury would prove no obstacle to her great dreams. After a hunting accident where she shot herself dead in the foot while climbing over a fence, she was undeterred and instead found ways around this newfound disability.

After her university years at Radcliffe College, Barnard College and then Colombia University where she studied French, German, Italian and economics she went off to Europe to finish her education. She spent many months trying to fulfill her dream to become a diplomat at the United States Foreign Service. She aced all the tests, surprising everyone by getting 100% in her oral diplomat exam, only to be rejected over and over again. She was eventually told that there was a policy against disabled people. This was, however, perfectly untrue: There were various male diplomats with prosthetic legs.

Virginia decided that if she couldn't be a diplomat and work for the Americans, she would go on to France and offer her help there. They said yes, and for a time she drove an ambulance for them delivering medicine to the ten million people that were fleeing Hitler's tanks.

After six weeks of driving the ambulance, she decided to go back to Britain and offer her services to the British Army. On the journey to Britain, in August of 1940, at a railway station, she was approached by George Bellows, an undercover British agent. He noticed her "force of personality" and struck up a conversation with her. He knew almost at once that this kind of chance doesn't come along often, and gave her the phone number of a friend that he said she should call once she reached London. This man was no ordinary friend; he was a senior official of the Special Operations Executive (SOE), the British espionage agency. She went to dinner with this "friend" and was recruited right then and there. And so it was that Virginia decided she would become a spy.

When Virginia Hall took on the operation to get 12 spies out of an internment camp in what would be one of the most daring rescues of the war, few believed that she could achieve the titanic task. That didn't matter though; she knew her own power, and would never stop until the mission was accomplished.

One morning in the spring of 1942 at the Grand Nouvel Hotel in Lyon, Virginia met Gaby Bloch; she was immediately impressed by this small French woman who was clearly braver than most men she had ever met. Gaby was the wife of former French deputy

Jean Pierre-Bloch who had been arrested with the rest of "Clan Cameron" as they were known by the SOE (Special Operations Executive), and sent to Périgueux. This prison in southwest France was at once freezing and damp. There was barely water, the prisoners were given oily sludge once a day to eat, and they were only allowed 10 minutes outside a day in the freezing winter. One of the men, Lieutenant Jumeau, described it as "degrading and humiliating to the last degree."

SOE was eager for an escape. The Camerons were "star agents" with expertise ranging from wireless transmitting, weapons and sabotage. It was of paramount importance to prevent them from being executed or worse, handed over to Hitler as trophy prisoners. This was the spring of 1942, WWII was raging on, and Gaby and the Camerons had lost faith in the SOE's periodical efforts to secure their release.

This wouldn't be Virginia's first prison break and these men knew that; they had heard about the women with piercing eyes and a limping leg that had helped Gerry Morel (a prisoner they had met at the filthy Périgueux) escape and he had told them that it was mostly due to the ingenuity of Virginia Hall. That brings us back to the smokey cafe in Lyon where these two shrewd and unimaginably brave women were seated facing each other. Gaby explained the efforts she had put in lobbying ministers in Vichy and that no one was listening to the small distraught Jewish woman. Virginia understood. She fully appreciated the magnitude of the problem. This prison was an "impenetrable stronghold of high walls and iron gates" that "no one escaped from."

So Virginia got to work. She devised a plan and told Baker Street that she was going to give this a go. London had little faith she could actually do it but she and Gaby were an unstoppable force dead-set on freeing the Camerons from the clutches of Nazi captivity.

First, Virginia tried to appeal to the American Admiral Leahy arguing that these were "symbolically important prisoners" and that the Americans and the British were allies in this war. There was only one problem: she could not reveal they were secret agents facing trial and most likely execution — that was classified.

Perhaps Leahy was concerned about bad press if he ignored her pleas or maybe Virginia was at her most persuasive. Her efforts were in vain, however, and it was soon announced that the prisoners were going to be moved from the stink of Périgueux to the internment camp at Mauzac in southwestern France.

Virginia considered this a good thing. Mauzac was in the countryside, the conditions were better and the men were going to be living in a hut outside. But of course there were many cons: Virginia was well known in those parts so she couldn't get close and the prison was armed to the teeth with cruel guards, surrounded by two barbed-wire fences and was encircled by watchtowers. This is where Gaby came in. Virginia supplied her with a load of bribe money and taught her techniques on how to recruit guards to help relay messages.

Jose Sevilla was the first guard recruit, in exchange for being taken to London to join the Free French, he would make sure that Watchtower Five (the one nearest to the men's hut) would remain unmanned at night and smuggled as many messages as he could to the Camerons. But even with his help, Virginia needed a more reliable way to communicate with them and to get them supplies.

Armed with money to buy black-market groceries and her convincing act of devastated and distressed wife, Gaby got them jam with a file at the bottom of the jar, some laundry with wire cutters hidden inside, hollowed out books with a screwdriver and hammer, lots of tins of sardines chosen for the very useful reusable metal and maybe most importantly: bread.

Every night the Camerons had "choir practice" and sang as loud as they could to drown out the noises that one of the men was making hammering the door of the barracks and making a mold of the key with bread. This was not enough though, there was a desperate need for clearer communication; the guards passing sporadic messages was not cutting it. So Virginia came up with a plan to send in an old French priest, a veteran of WWI who had lost both his legs, under the guise of bringing pastoral visits to the prisoners.

The priest at first brought them some paint to "spruce up their hut" and when this hut make-over was finished, he asked to be taken there to see how it turned out. Finally inside the hut with the men, he said to them excitedly "one of you look under my cassock." He had smuggled in a transmitter disguised as a piano. Now there was a direct line in and out of the prison — London was practically gobsmacked at this feat of subterfuge.

With the escape plans now almost complete, the men tested the makeshift key they had made from the bread mold, but to their utter horror, it didn't work. The choir began again while a new key was hammered into existence. This time they got it right, which was a saving grace as their limited time was rapidly dwindling. They needed to get out during the new moon, the only time it was dark enough to not get caught.

On July 15, the men waited anxiously for the all clear sign: if they were good to go, an old lady would pass by the camp; if the plan was called off, an old man would walk by. Thankfully, at the given time a little old lady inconspicuously walked by.

The men went to work stuffing rags under the blankets to make them look as if they were all asleep. The watchtower was clear and the lock worked this time. Once opened, they immediately hung a painted sackcloth that had been made to look like a door and sped through the wire using an old carpet. At that moment, a guard came. They froze in place, but then the guard whispered: "Well don't make so much noise." And so with that, the men made the rest of the journey under the barbed wire in exactly 12 minutes: a minute a man.

Once they were out, Virginia had made meticulous plans for them to get to a safe house stocked with groceries, clothes and beds for the first and most crucial hours of the escape and then to get them all back to London.

She had done it — she had gotten 12 of the most important spies out of a so-called impenetrable internment camp and back to safety, and officially became an SOE legend. The historian M.R.D

Foot wrote that this jailbreak was "one of the war's most useful operations of its kind." Hitler was furious.

After the Mauzac escape she became one of the most important Allied spies of the war. She went on to blow up bridges and tunnels and "tricked, traded, and like 007, had a license to kill." At one point she had to escape the Nazis, and her only way to do this was to cross the Pyrenees mountains in the dead of winter with barely any food or proper clothes, all on foot while her prosthetic leg gushed blood.

After the war was over, Virginia went back home to Baltimore, and she was awarded the Distinguished Service Cross by none other than the famous William Donovan. Instead of marrying into a life of luxury as her mother had wished, she became one of the CIA's first female intelligence agents.

Robert F. Kennedy once said "It is from numberless diverse acts of courage and belief that human history is shaped. Each time a man stands up for an ideal, or acts to improve the lot of other, or strikes out against injustice, he sends forth a tiny ripple of hope...." Virginia's many acts as a spy were absolutely essential to defeating the Nazis, and we all owe our freedom today to the courage of people like the "Limping Lady."

Virginia Hall passed away on July 12, 1982 in Rockville, Maryland at the age of 76.

Source:

https://ee.usembassy.gov/wp-content/uploads/sites/207/Not-Bad-for-a-Girl-from-Baltimore.pdf

A Woman Of No Importance' Finally Gets Her Due

https://www.npr.org/2019/04/18/711356336/a-woman-of-no-importance-finally-gets-her-due

https://www.cia.gov/stories/story/virginia-hall-the-courage-and-daring-of-the-limping-lady/

"You don't make progress by standing on the sidelines, whimpering and complaining. You make progress by implementing ideas."

— Shirley Chisholm

Ruby Bradley

I used to tell everyone in that POW camp to try to roll with the punches. When we were faced with eating worms to survive, I'd say, 'Aha! Protein! I will eat for the good of my country.

Ruby Bradley was born in 1907 and raised on a farm in West Virginia. After college, her first job was teaching in a small schoolhouse. During the Great Depression, Bradley observed that many of her students lacked food. She made it an everyday responsibility to bring extra food for her students. Many times, she remembered her students would take their portions home to share with their families.

After spending a day with her sister, who was working as a Walter Reed General Hospital nurse, Bradley determined that being a nurse was her life's passion. She was accepted into Philadelphia General Hospital in the early 1930s. After graduating from nursing school, she joined the Army Nurse Corps in 1934.

This decision marked the beginning of a remarkable journey that would lead her to serve in multiple conflicts, including World War II, the Korean War, and the Vietnam War. Bradley remembered fondly her recruiter telling her, "Don't worry; you won't be in any war!"

In January 1940, the Army assigned her to a hospital on the island of Corregidor. Known for its rocky terrain, was strategically located at the entrance of Manila Bay, just south of Bataan province, Philippines.

Bradley was then ordered to Baguio in February 1941. Baguio is known as the "Summer Capital of the Philippines" due to its lower temperatures —it is five thousand feet above sea level. There, Bradley worked as the chief nurse and a surgical assistant.

Just after the Pearl Harbor attack in early December, Japanese planes strafed and bombed Baguio. The wounded came in large waves into the camp's hospital. For the next two weeks, Bradley and her staff worked day and night, except for brief moments when they took refuge in bunkers during further attacks.

On the morning of December 23, 1941, after assisting in thirty-seven operations, the hospital received information of an imminent attack and was ordered to move the camp immediately. Bradley helped pack up equipment and supplies. They loaded patients into all available vehicles and even utilized old-style wagons to attempt to flee into the mountains, but passage was impossible.

Now, three weeks after the Japanese military bombed Pearl Harbor, Bradley, just thirty-four years old, was captured as a prisoner of war. "The Japanese told us that if anyone escaped, five people would be shot. Three days after we were captured, we did an appendectomy, and the Japanese soldiers thought it was wonderful that we could do all this without instruments," recalled Bradley.

Treating patients without equipment took creativity and ingenuity, but Bradley became resourceful. She used a tea strainer and gauze to anesthetize a pregnant woman who went into labor. They made their own lye from fats mixed into charcoal wood ashes when their meager supply of soap ran out. "I used to tell everyone to roll with the punches. When we were faced with worms, I'd say, 'Aha! Protein! I will eat for the good of my country," added Bradley.

After being transferred to the Santo Tomas internment camp in Manila in September 1943, several patients died every day. The

POWs lived on half a cup of rice in the morning and another at night. In the squalor and unsanitary conditions, Bradley lost twenty-five pounds. Most of her weight loss was due to her, once again, refusing to allow children to go hungry and giving her food rations to the starving local population's children.

Bradley used the extra space in her now-baggy clothes to conceal and smuggle medical supplies into the camp. "I was a pretty good thief," Bradley stated.

In February 1945, US troops finally broke through enemy lines and liberated the camp. During her thirty-seven months of captivity, Bradley assisted in 230 significant operations and the delivery of eighteen babies.

After her liberation, Bradley returned to the United States and was eventually promoted to major. In July 1950, during the Korean War, Bradley took over as chief nurse for the 171st Evacuation Hospital.

The hospital's position required constant shifting as the front lines changed.

In November of 1950, the North Korean Army, backed by 100,000 Chinese Communist troops, advanced toward the 38th Parallel.

Bradley's Hospital, the 171st Evac, stood directly in their path. Bradley sent her subordinates out on planes with the first round of the most critically wounded and stayed to supervise the withdrawal of the remaining patients.

Several of the convoys to the airstrip were ambushed as communist troops armed with snipers tried to inflict maximum casualties. "Everything was happening real fast," Bradley said in an interview.

Bradley was the last person to jump aboard an awaiting plane. Enemy snipers surrounded the plane. The abandoned ambulance that had transported Bradley was destroyed by the explosion of an enemy shell, which barely missed her plane. Bradley later opined about the incident, "You can get out in a hurry when there's somebody behind you with a gun!" The North Korean Army achieved its mission by dividing the North from the South.

In 1951, Bradley was named chief nurse for the Eighth Army. She supervised 500 front-line nurses throughout Korea. When she left in 1953, she was the first woman to be given a full-dress honor guard ceremony.

In 1958, Bradley was promoted to colonel, making her only the third woman in US Army history to achieve the rank. Bradley retired in 1963 as the most highly decorated woman in the history of the US Army, with 34 awards and decorations, including two Legion of Merit medals, two Bronze Stars, the Korean Service Medal with one silver and two bronze stars, and the Red Cross's prestigious Florence Nightingale Medal. Bradley spent the next seventeen years supervising a private-duty nursing service in Roane County.

Ruby Bradley passed away in 2002 at age 94. She was laid to rest in Arlington National Cemetery, with a complete military ceremonial firing party of seven sounding three volleys in her honor, Bradley's flag-draped coffin escorted by six horses to her final resting site.

Source:

Raquel Lohe – Simple Cremation. https://simplecremation.us/raquel-lohe/

Corregidor Island, Cavite City, Southern Luzen, Philippines - GibSpain. https://gibspain.com/listing/corregidor-island-cavite-city-southern-luzen-philippines/

"The future belongs to those who believe in the beauty of their dreams."

— Eleanor Roosevelt

Jane Kendeigh

"Among the Americans Who Served on Iwo Jima, Uncommon Valor was a common virtue, and I cannot think of a better example than Ensign Jane Kendeigh, who was willing to risk her life every day if it meant others would be able to see the next."

— *Fleet Admiral Chester W. Nimitz*

The Battle of Iwo Jima, from February 19 to March 26, 1945, was one of the most grueling battles during World War II. This small, volcanic island in the Pacific became the stage for an epic confrontation between the US Marine Corps and the Japanese Army. The ferocity of the fighting, the inhospitable terrain, and the sheer determination of both sides made Iwo Jima a defining moment in the War.

As dawn broke on February 19, 1945, thousands of US Marines stormed the sandy beaches of Iwo Jima, only to be met with a deadly silence. The Japanese, well-entrenched in underground bunkers and miles of interconnected tunnels, waited patiently before unleashing a devastating arsenal of artillery, machine guns, and mortar fire. The beach quickly turned into a nightmare-killing ground, with US Marines struggling through soft volcanic ash that slowed their movement, leaving them vulnerable to enemy fire.

The battle raged on as the US Marines pushed forward, inch by bloody inch, against a deeply entrenched and fanatical enemy. The Japanese commander, Lieutenant General Kuribayashi, had devised a strategy of attrition, ensuring that every one of his soldiers fought to their last breath. Unlike previous Pacific battles, where large unit banzai charges were a hallmark of Japanese resistance, Kuribayashi's men engaged in calculated, organized defense, making the American advance painfully slow and deadly.

One of the most grueling battles occurred at Mount Suribachi, the highest point on the island. This dormant volcano served as a critical higher-ground vantage point for the Japanese military, allowing them to rain accurate and intense fire upon the advancing Marines. On February 23rd, after four days of brutal combat, US forces finally secured the summit, raising the American flag captured in an iconic photograph by Joe Rosenthal. However, while this moment symbolized a victory for US forces, the battle was far from over.

The central and northern parts of the island witnessed some of the most brutal and desperate fighting. Locations such as the Meat Grinder, Turkey Knob, and Hill 382 became infamous for their carnage. The Marines faced relentless machine-gun nests, booby traps, and hidden snipers, forcing them to engage in savage, close-quarters combat. Flamethrowers and explosives became essential tools in clearing out Japanese positions buried deep within the island's rocky terrain.

The battle for Iwo Jima lasted over a month, with every inch of ground taken at an immense, deadly cost. The Japanese, refusing to surrender, fought until almost all of their 21,000 defenders were killed. The US forces suffered greatly as well, with close to 7,000 Marines killed and over 19,000 wounded. In the end, Iwo Jima was secured, providing a crucial airfield for American bombers and a testament to the extraordinary resilience and sacrifice of those who fought there.

During this fierce fighting, the US military needed medical personnel on the battlefield to nurse those who were wounded and take care of their casualties to ensure victory. Thus, the first female Navy flight nurses program was created, and among that crew was the first female flight nurse to fly into an active combat zone in the Pacific Combat. The courageous twenty-two-year-old Ensign Jane "Candy" Kendeigh came on board.

Jane Louise Kendeigh was born to Earl Samuel Kendi and Olive Mata Bates in Henrietta, Ohio, on March 30th, 1922, and was raised on an apple orchard farm. As far as she could remember, she always wanted to help those in need and become a nurse.

She began her quest by graduating from the St. Luke School of Nursing in 1943 and joining the US Naval Nurse Corps shortly thereafter. Ultimately, she aimed to rescue wounded soldiers sent to distant lands during World War II. Her dream was to save those who were engaged in saving the nation.

She then became one of the twelve nurses who comprised the first group to volunteer for training as air evacuation flight nurses in the US Navy. Kendeigh and her fellow classmates were trained to treat patients at high altitudes and other critical medical situations unique to flying. They received training in plane crash procedures and field survival and even learned how to fight in hand-to-hand combat if needed.

During the water crash landing training, knowing how to swim wasn't enough to survive and pass the course. Flight nurses also had to demonstrate endurance, speed, and the ability to tow a victim for a specified distance.

A press release at that time would describe her as "one-hundred-eight pounds of green-eyed charm and efficiency." Kendeigh wasn't just tough; she was among the first Navy nurses to finish flight training and travel to the Pacific.

On January 22nd, 1945, Kendeigh and eleven other nurses were assigned to the one Squadron. Women were just starting to gain official military positions during this same time.

On March 6, 1945, Kendeigh's actions would go down in history. At 2:00 a.m., Ensign Kendeigh boarded a large C-47 in Guam headed for Iwo Jima. Also on the plane was US Navy photographer Lieutenant Gill Dewitt, tasked with documenting the first Navy nurse in action.

When the plane arrived at Iwo Jima, they discovered the airfield was under attack. The C-47 circled overhead, looking for a break in the fighting. "We circled and circled the small island, watching the bursting shells beneath us like firecrackers on a fourth of July," Navy photographer Dewitt later said.

Finally, as the fighting started to slow down, the C-47 could land despite the enemy continuing to drop heavy mortar fire near the landing strip.

Upon landing, Kendeigh exited the plane and quickly made her way to a field hospital as mortars exploded all around her. She and the medics prepared sixteen wounded soldiers for the return flight. "We took the worst, the ones that could not wait. Others would later be evacuated on hospital ships," Kendeigh told reporters.

Finally, the C-47 was back in the air, and the pilot asked Kendeigh if she'd been scared. "I don't remember being frightened while we were on the ground," Kendeigh responded. "There wasn't time to think about anything except getting these wounded men on board. But now we are safe; in the air again, I find my knees are shaking, so I can hardly stand up."

In that fateful mission, Jane Kendeigh became the first flight nurse to land in an active combat zone, and Journalist Gil Dewitt was with her to record it. He was right in position to take an infamous photograph of her in action treating the wounded. She later became known as the most whistled-at nurse in the Pacific. The photo of her nursing wounded soldiers made the front page of newspapers nationwide.

However, instead of celebrating her accomplishment and straying from her mission, Kendeigh rolled up her sleeves and returned to work. For the next two weeks, Kendeigh and her fellow nurses would fly in and out of Iwo Jima, evacuating nearly twenty-four hundred severely injured US Marines and soldiers back to relative safety.

Thanks to the care of nurses like Kendeigh, only forty-six died en route to the hospital. After the end of World War II, flight nurses stayed on hand to retrieve freed prisoners of War after their wartime confinement.

Barbara Miller Finch, a worker correspondent who once traveled with Kendeigh on the same plane, recalled watching her work. "Kendeigh first acquainted herself with the needs of each case and spoke to each man, building a rapport with them. She made a mental chart of the condition of each of the twenty wounded men on that flight, which she perfectly recited to me as I asked about their condition," Finch added.

In another particular instance highlighting her attentiveness to her patients, a young US Marine, William Wykoff, was lying on a stretcher in the hospital, dazed and in poor health. As he lay on the stretcher, he suddenly saw flashing lights popping in front of him.

"I tried to jump off the stretcher. I thought it was another attack until I heard this woman's voice. I was so shocked to hear a woman's voice in the middle of all this death and destruction. That woman was Ensign Kendeigh, who told me, 'Don't worry, Marine, you are safe; it's only those pesky Navy photographers.' Wykoff wasn't exactly sure where he was, and his vision was hampered by his injuries. He said, "I only knew I was on Iwo Jima, but then there she was, an angel in fatigues beside me, and it lifted my spirits."

Kendeigh took care of Wykoff that day, and during that mission, she worked tirelessly for fifteen days straight until all of her patients were safely transported to ambulances in Guam.

Back at home in the US, Kendeigh was becoming a bit of a media sensation. When she left Iwo Jima, she returned to the US and helped with the critical War bond drive. Her heart, however, was with her work back in the Pacific, and she asked to go back.

On April 7, 1945, she was among the first flight nurses to fly into Okinawa, Japan. She made a total of six flights to Okinawa, rescuing and evacuating the soldiers on that small island once again and carving out a new piece of history.

Lieutenant General Kuribayashi would say about the fighting at Iwo Jima, "America's productive powers are beyond our imagination. Japan has started a War with a formidable enemy, and we must brace ourselves accordingly." Kuribayshi earlier recognized that the Japanese military could not hold Iwo Jima against the American onslaught.

"The raising of that flag on Suribachi means a Marine Corps for the next five hundred years." — James Forrestal, Secretary of the US Navy 1944

Jane Kendeigh survived the War and returned home. As so many in the Greatest Generation would do, she set aside the horrors of what she'd seen and did her best to resume a regular life. She couldn't forget the faces of all those she treated, though, and was proud of her time in the military.

Kendeigh later married US Navy Lieutenant Robert Cheverton, an air evacuation pilot. They wedded on Valentine's Day, 1946, in San Marino, California. The couple had three daughters, and Kendeigh continued to work as a nurse, but this time at a doctor's office in San Diego.

On February 22, 1986, Kendeigh and her family were invited to an Iwo Jima reunion. To her surprise, Kendeigh was asked to come on the stage. A man was brought out to her on a stretcher, reenacting what occurred over forty years earlier.

Initially thinking the man on the stretcher was just an actor, Kendeigh looked down and was shocked. The man was US Marine Sergeant William Wykoff, the young man disturbed by the photographer's flashbulbs. For Wykoff, it would indeed be the first time he could see one of his angels in fatigues as, according to a San Diego Union-Tribune article, he couldn't see her that first day as his vision was impaired by a grenade blast. Sadly, Sergeant William Wykoff would pass away only two years later in 1998.

When asked by a reporter at the reunion about her feelings about the lack of recognition the Navy Nurses received during World War II, Kendeigh responded, "Our rewards are the warm smiles, a slow nod of appreciation, a gesture, a word—accolades that are greater and more heart-warming than any medal or commendation."

At only sixty-five, Jane Kendeigh sadly passed away on July 19th, 1987, in San Diego, California. Her heroic deeds and patriotism will never be forgotten. Her service remains the epitome of the courage, tenacity, and sacrifice of the women who served during World War II. Her role was no less challenging and harrowing than thousands of others, yet every bit as heroic.

Today, the incredible accounts of the brave women of Iwo Jima and Okinawa remain a minor footnote in military history; these women never achieved any medals for their service, let alone much notoriety. God bless the brave flight nurses who gave their all!

Source:

This Day in History: The first Navy flight nurse. https://www.taraross.com/post/tdih-jane-kendeigh

Iwo Jima, 1944, USMC, WWII Battle Map | Battlemaps.us. https://www.battlemaps.us/products/iwo-jima-1944-45-usmc-wwii-map

Nancy Grace Augusta Wake

New Zealand's Nancy Grace Augusta Wake was a rebel, a spy, and a highly decorated World War II resistance fighter. Wake earned the nickname "The White Mouse" from the Nazi higher-ups, and a five million franc bounty was placed on her head. She defied the Nazi's, outran all her enemies, and lived to the ripe old age of 98 to tell her tale.

Wake was born in Wellington, New Zealand, on August 30, 1912. Her family moved to Sydney, Australia, where she attended school. At only sixteen years old, she ran away from home and found work as a nurse. In 1932, a financial windfall and strong wanderlust for adventure enabled her to leave Australia for a new life in Europe.

Wake settled in Paris, working as a news reporter for the Hearst group of newspapers. As the 1930s progressed, the rise of German fascism formed the basis of many of Wake's opinions. In 1935, she traveled to Berlin and Vienna, where she witnessed horrific violence and anti-Semitism. She quickly vowed to oppose Nazism by any means.

In November 1939, she would find love and marry Henri Fiocca, a wealthy industrialist. Six months after their wedding, the country of Germany embarked on its dark visions of conquest by invading France. After France's surrender, Wake and Fiocca would risk their lives by joining the fledgling Resistance.

With Wake's growing involvement in the Resistance, she and her husband assisted the escape of Allied service members and Jewish refugees from France into neutral Spain. Fearful of being captured, Wake fled Marseilles, and after a brief period of imprisonment, she made her escape across the Pyrenees. In June 1943, she reached England, where she began working in the Special Operations Executive (SOE).

Formed in 1940, the SOE was an underground spy network that waged a secret war in enemy-held territories throughout Asia and Europe. Its agents demonstrated incredible courage and resourcefulness by utilizing the guerrilla warfare tactics of hit and run. By working with resistance forces, they boosted the morale of occupied territories.

After a short training period, Wake returned to France in April 1944 to help build and train the Resistance before D-Day. Working in the Auvergne region, Wake organized parachute drops of military weapons and equipment. After D-Day, Wake was involved in combat with elements of various German troops sent to destroy the Maquis.

Upon liberation, Wake learned that her husband, Henri, had been killed by the Gestapo in August 1943. In September of 1944, she left the Resistance and went to work in the SOE headquarters in Paris.

After the war, Wake received medals and commendations from the United States, Britain, and France. Her restless, wanderlust spirit and post-traumatic stress prevented her from adapting to life in post-war Europe. In January of 1949, at only thirty-seven years old, she returned to Australia.

Wake returned to England eight years later and married John Forward, an RAF Officer. The couple returned to Australia in 1959. In December 2001, she left Australia for England, where she lived out her remaining years.

For her courageous endeavors, she received the George Medal, the 1939-45 Star, the France and Germany Star, the Defense Medal, the British War Medal 1939-45, the French Officer of the Legion of Honour, the French Croix de Guerre with a Star and two Palms, the US Medal for Freedom with a Palm, and the French Medaille de la Resistance.

Source:

Nancy Wake (1st Edition) – Welcome to Regimental Books. https://regimental-books.com.au/product/nancy-wake/

Catherine Leroy with John Deangelis in Hue City during the "Tet Offensive." Photo take by US Marine Ryan Thomas.

Catherine Leroy

Catherine Leroy was an award-winning war photographer and ground-breaking journalist whose harrowing combat pictures illustrated the true story of the Vietnam War, brandishing the covers of LIFE magazine and other media.

Catherine Leroy was born in France on August 27, 1944. After seeing images of the war, she decided to travel to South Vietnam to "give war a human face." In 1966, at only twenty-one years old, she booked a one-way ticket to Laos with her old Leica-M2 35 mm camera and just two hundred dollars in her pocket. Leroy had no idea what she was getting herself into. Despite having no military experience or even basic knowledge of photography, Leroy was determined to make her mark as a world-class combat photojournalist.

Upon her arrival in Saigon via Laos, Leroy met photographer Horst Faas, bureau chief of the Associated Press. After lying about her photography experience, Leroy was given three rolls of film and the offer that if any of the photos were usable, she would be paid fifteen US dollars each.

At that time, Leroy was the only female photojournalist working during the Vietnam War. This was just after the death of reporter Dickey Chapelle, who was killed by a grenade in 1965.

A year later, on February 23, 1967, Leroy became the first accredited journalist to participate in a combat parachute jump, joining the 173rd Airborne Brigade in Operation Junction City.

Leroy was so small that she had to be weighed down with machine gun parts so she wouldn't descend too slowly and be blown too far away from the rest of the company. "I was swimming in my size six jungle boots, but I thought the jump was fantastic. I was even able to take some pictures while I jumped, " said Leroy in a CSPAN-recorded interview.

Leroy got into hot water and her press credentials were temporarily suspended after she yelled at a Marine Corps officer who she felt was condescending when denying her request to parachute jump after Operation Junction City.

Barely two months after her parachute jump, Leroy was on the ground covering the Hill Fights near Khe Sanh. Historians place those as some of the bloodiest and hardest-fought battles during the Vietnam War.

On April 30th, 1967, US Marines moved from Hill 861 to support entrenched Marines and walked into an enemy bunker complex, suffering nine killed and forty-three wounded. Later that day, the 3rd and 9th Marines began assaulting Hill 881 South. They were hit by mortar and heavy machine gun fire from numerous well-concealed enemy bunkers.

The Marines were pinned down and could only disengage after several hours with gunship and air support. The Marines suffered forty-three killed and 109 wounded in the engagement, while the enemy losses were 163 killed.

That May 1967, Leroy's dramatic pictures of Navy Corpsman Vernon Wike attending a mortally injured Marine on Hill 881 appeared as a *Paris Match* story. The photos were also published in *LIFE* magazine to critical acclaim.

In the photos— one of three taken in quick succession—Wike is kneeling in tall grass, holding a US Marine who had just been shot, while smoke from the battle rises into the background. In the first frame, Wike has two hands on the Marine's chest, trying to staunch the wound. In the second, he is trying to find a heartbeat.

In the third frame, "Corpsman In Anguish," he has just realized the man had passed away.

Nine months later, in February 1968, Leroy went on to make *LIFE*'s cover story with her photographs and, a rare feat, her own words telling the short time she spent as a prisoner of North Vietnamese forces near Hué during the Têt Offensive.

On May 19, 1967, while photographing Operation Hickory with a Marine unit near the Vietnamese Demilitarized Zone, Leroy was severely injured by enemy mortar fire. Leroy would later credit a camera with saving her life by stopping some of the shrapnel. She was evacuated first to Con Thien, then to the USS *Sanctuary*, where III Marine Amphibious Force Commander General Lew Walt visited her. She was then transferred to a hospital in Danang and discharged in mid-June.

In September 1967, she photographed the siege of Con Thien. In 1968, during the Tet Offensive, Leroy and Agence France-Presse journalist Francois Mazure were captured by enemy soldiers during the Battle of Huê. With the assistance of a priest who was under house arrest to interpret for her, Leroy managed to talk her way out of her captivity.

Transcribed from her *LIFE* magazine story, Leroy gives her recollection of the incident.

★★★

We were pedaling our rickety bicycle right into the outskirts of Huê before the bullets started popping all around, and we realized just how much trouble we were in. François Mazure, a correspondent for Agence France Presse, and I had started out that morning from the Marine base at Phu Bai to find out about the fighting.

We hitchhiked a ride with an American convoy to a point about four miles south of the city. We hadn't seen any sign of the Marines a general had told us would be guarding the road, so we changed into civilian clothes we had brought along just in case this kind of situation arose. We had rented the old bicycle from a French-speaking Vietnamese who lived along the road and continued north riding tandem.

The road was empty now, and the people were hiding in their houses. We were growing nervous, and whenever we did see people peering from their houses, François called "bonjour, bonjour," very loud and friendly, to show that we were French and not American. We reached the edge of the city and passed a big marketplace. And that's when the shooting started. People were standing about in little knots, and we walked up to them shouting in French, "French press from Paris," but they wouldn't look at us.

We stayed in the marketplace for about two hours while the shooting continued, and South Vietnamese fighter-bombers flew air strikes against the walled citadel of Huê about a mile to the north. We realized by now that we were in a part of the city controlled by the Communists. Finally, a man directed us to a nearby cathedral where he thought we might be safe.

The cathedral and the grounds around it swarmed with refugees from the two days of fighting in the city. François kept saying, "French press," but the people did not look happy to see us. Hundreds of children surrounded us. They were silent and wide-eyed and hostile, and they pressed against us, pushing in from all sides.

I was glad when a priest arrived. He was a good-looking Vietnamese man of about forty who spoke French with great elegance and precision. He told us we were welcome to stay the night, and the priest showed us around the cathedral and grounds.

There were about four thousand refugees, most of them women, children, and old men. There were about ten wounded, and one woman had just given birth to a baby. She lay on the floor in front of a confessional. Inside, the sound of all the people talking and the children crying was incredible, a rolling, continuous roar. That night, we slept in the priest's room—or tried to.

Next door, in another room, all the priests were praying loudly in Vietnamese, and their prayers were punctuated by bursts of gunfire.

The next morning, the priest told us flatly that the people were unhappy about us being there. They feared that our presence, as whites, might enrage the North Vietnamese. A young boy, a former juvenile delinquent with whom the priest had been working, volunteered to try to lead us through the North Vietnamese lines to the military compound where the Americans were holding out.

We left all our military clothes behind, even our boots. I got a pair of priest's sandals, François a pair of shower shoes. I stuffed my American and Vietnamese military identity cards in my bra, along with several cans of film that were already exposed.

I am only five feet tall and weigh sixty-five pounds, and I kept asking François, an old friend, 'Look at my bosom; does it look strange?' We made a white flag from one of the priest's robes and made two big signs saying "French press" and pinned them across our shirts.

The priest himself wrote a letter for us in Vietnamese, explaining who we were. Then we started down the trail from the church, our young delinquent out ahead of us with the white flag.

We soon came to a large, pleasant-looking villa with a garden around it, and suddenly, we realized uniformed men were standing there staring at us. They looked astonished. The boy waved his white flag furiously, and we started shouting what was becoming our password "French Press!" Three men came up to us. They were North Vietnamese soldiers. They were dressed in khaki uniforms and carried AK-47 automatic rifles. Their faces were hostile, but they seemed calm. I was less afraid now than before.

At least the three men were real; you could see them and smell them. They were somehow less frightening than the enemy with no face, the only one I had known before.

François handed them the letter from the priest. They looked at it but did not seem to be reading it. They just stared at the paper. I saw François clutch his camera the photographer's reflex was taking over. But the men took our cameras away and motioned us

133

toward the garden. At the gate, they tied our hands behind our backs with parachute cords. They were being thorough rather than brutal.

They led us into the garden, and we saw about fifteen soldiers sitting in foxholes dug under the trees. Several of them came up and looked at us impassively. François had retrieved the letter. He held it in his bound hands, and each time a man approached him, he twisted around and presented the letter. They just looked at the paper but never read it.

We stood in the garden for about an hour. François kept talking to them very angrily in French. In order not to seem frightened, apprehensive, or guilty, he acted as if he were offended and furious at being made to suffer such indignities.

Overhead, an American spotter plane and a Vietnamese bomber circled. Each time they came over, François and I dove to the dirt. The North Vietnamese seemed unconcerned about the aircraft and hardly moved.

At last, we were taken to a small building in the back of the house, apparently the servants' quarters. When we walked in, we saw a heavy-set white man, about fifty years old, with a worried face. "Are you French?' François burst out. "Yes, yes I am," the big man answered. He seemed terribly glad to see us, and we were just as happy to see him. We even turned halfway around so that he could shake our bound hands. Almost nothing will stop a Frenchman from shaking hands.

The man told us an extraordinary story. He managed the electricity plant in the area. A year ago, while out driving at night, he was ambushed by the Vietcong, and shot. One of the bullets had severed two of his fingers.

When the Vietcong rushed up to the car to finish him off, he screamed, "I am a Frenchman. Please don't kill me." The Vietcong leader bandaged his wounded hand, helped him to get his car started, and released him. Then, two nights later, the North Vietnamese had come, screaming in waves across the rice fields, and taken over the Frenchman's house. Several Viet Cong political agents arrived to talk with their comrades, and, incredibly, their leader was the same VC who had ambushed him a few days before.

The VC soldier greeted the Frenchman cordially and decided what to do. The Frenchman, his Vietnamese wife, and two teenage daughters would be kept prisoners in their own home. All in all, the Frenchmen stated that the North Vietnamese had treated them quite well.

As we sat talking, a new soldier entered, a North Vietnamese officer. When the Frenchman's wife told him who we were, the officer ordered his men to untie us. With the Frenchman's wife translating, the young officer told us that they held the city now and had expelled the Americans. When we asked if we could take some pictures, he agreed and escorted us outside. He seemed very pleased with himself and acted like some of the Public Relations officers I've met in American units.

The men seemed to be delighted at having their pictures taken. The only trouble was that they always wanted to strike those phony-looking heroic poses you see in North Vietnamese propaganda pictures. One grabbed a grenade and made it as if to throw it. Another held up an American M-79 grenade launcher.

Only one man objected to being photographed. He was a soldier holding an American military radio, and when he saw I'd shot him with a telephoto lens, he came over and demanded my film. I had no intention of giving it up and instead managed to hand him a perfectly blank roll of unexposed film.

We pretended to be most casual, as if running around with North Vietnamese regulars was old stuff to us. But the fighting was raging all around us, sometimes very close. At any minute, the government troops or the Americans might come driving in, and there we'd be in the middle of a firefight. When we returned to the house, François remarked, very off handedly and cleverly, "Well, we have to get back to Paris with our story, so we'll be running along now."

The officer didn't object at all. The Frenchman passed out cigars to François and the officer, and they all lit up. Then we shook hands gaily with all the officers and said goodbye to the

French family. With our young Vietnamese guide, we started out the gate. We looked back and saw the Frenchman standing with his wife and daughters. He waved at us slowly, and his eyes were very wet.

When we reached the cathedral again, all the priests and people swarmed around us, asking questions, and the boy proudly told them what had happened. François and I were laughing crazily, and all the people were laughing, too.

Their hostility was gone, and they were saying in English, "Number one, number one." They took us to a room, and suddenly, the room was full of food. After the meal, we gave our young guide two thousand piasters, roughly seventeen US dollars, and asked what he wanted from Paris. He laughed and said he wanted a pair of blue jeans.

We were ready to leave. Our troubles were not over yet: We had yet to walk back through the North Vietnamese and through the no man's land. I said again and again, "François, I'll kiss the first two Americans I meet!"

We ended up finding an ARVN compound where there were two wounded Americans. I tried to find some morphine while François worked on the radio. Finally, he got a Medevac chopper to come and pick them up. We hunkered down there during a fierce firefight and eventually got back to the US military compound.

The next morning, we accompanied an American unit on a sweep. I saw a US Marine mechanized Ontos, which sort of looks like a tank, and shoot six recoilless rifles following our group as protection.

The next thing you know, we are in front of that same church, and all of a sudden, bullets start flying. The Marines are now shooting into the church, the same people we were sharing food with only a day before.

Because the North Vietnamese were all around and nobody knew who was who, I ran screaming to the Marine platoon leader, begging, "There are hundreds of refugees in there; they aren't VC, they are just civilians!" And those huge warriors in their flak jackets grinned down at me, acknowledging my words, and stopped shooting.

★★★

The subsequent story of Leroy's capture and escape made the cover of *LIFE* magazine and one of its featured articles about the war. During her three years in the war, Leroy wrote hundreds of letters to her family.

The letters were a testament to how she was processing the trauma of the war and navigating all the logistical challenges. They are candid and revealing, attesting to her resiliency, exposing her insecurities, and showing her moments of joy, despair, courage, and optimism.

In early 1968, Leroy was awarded the George Polk Award by the Overseas Press Club for her photos on Hill 881, becoming the first freelancer and first woman to win the award.

"When you look at war photographs, they seem to be silent moments of eternity. For me, they are haunted by sound, a deafening sound. The Vietnam War, most of the time, it was extremely boring, and exhausting. You walked for miles through rice paddies and jungles, crawling in the most unbearable circumstances. And nothing was happening. Then all of a sudden, all hell would break loose." —Catherine Leroy

Leroy's last major Vietnam photo essay, "This is That War," was published in *Look* magazine on May 14, 1968—the same issue when the editors changed policy to denounce the war.

In August 1972, Leroy and Frank Cavestani began filming *Operation Last Patrol*, a film about Ron Kovic and the anti-war Vietnam vets during their protests at the 1972 Republican National Convention in Miami. The film inspired Ron Kovic to write his autobiographical book, *Born on the Fourth of July*.

Leroy returned to Saigon in mid-April 1975, not as a reporter but to witness the fall of Saigon. On April 30th, she and Françoise Demulder photographed the North Vietnamese entering the city, and Demulder took the iconic photo of a tank crashing through the gate of the Independence Palace.

In 1976, Leroy covered the Lebanese Civil War. From 1977 to 1986, she covered conflicts in Northern Ireland, Cyprus, Somalia, Afghanistan, Iraq, and Iran and Libya for *Time Magazine*, and finally ended her war photography in the early 1990s.

Catherine Leroy passed away on July 8, 2006, in Santa Monica, California, one week after being diagnosed with lung cancer.

Source:

Female Correspondents of the Vietnam War – CherriesWriter – Vietnam War website. https://cherrieswriter.com/2016/06/21/female-correspondents-of-the-vietnam-war/?replytocom=84001

Vesma, G. (2022). Crossing the Frame: Western Women Photojournalists in Vietnam, 1961-1975. https://core.ac.uk/download/565369702.pdf

What is the most famous war photo? – Aliciapyne.com. https://aliciapyne.com/what-is-the-most-famous-war-photo/

Women in Combat

Leigh Anne Hester

I remember getting out of my truck, hearing the bullets whizz by, and pinging off of the concrete and puffs of dust around my feet. The funny thing is I don't remember how anything smelled, and I barely remember the gunshots. When you're involved in something like that, you don't even hear your own weapon.

When the smoke cleared, and I walked up out of the trench, and there was one of my guys laying there, bleeding out, saying I can't feel my legs, you know, it's a pretty sobering moment."

On March 20, 2005, just south of Baghdad and near the town of Salman Pak, Iraq, US Army Sergeant Leigh Anne Hester was serving as the team leader in a Military Police Brigade.

"It was early morning, and we went out as a nine-man squad, and it was our job to clear our Area of Operation of any roadside bombs; we didn't find any, and we didn't see any insurgents or anything like that. Then the convoys started coming through a few hours later, and we just happened to turn around on the right convoy, if you will, and then went through.

"They went down the road a little ways and we were following right behind them, and we just started hearing loud and close rapid gunfire, AK-47s, machine gun fire and explosions," said Sgt. Hester.

The supply train, consisting primarily of unarmored eighteen-wheelers driven by Iraqi and Turkish civilians, instantly found themselves under a heavy attack. The large enemy insurgent force was concealed in a row of irrigation ditches just off the side of the road.

One of the two American Humvee's escorting the convoy was knocked out almost immediately by rocket-propelled grenade fire. The second Hummvee pulled up and tried to mount a defense, but all three US soldiers were wounded by fire from the concealed enemy positions.

With the American soldiers sufficiently suppressed, a group of more than thirty insurgent fighters advanced on foot toward the convoy. As they ran forward, they started pulling out handcuffs to capture the wounded troops and bring them back as POW's. Sgt. Hester and her team that day were outnumbered five to one.

"In a split second, we decided that the best course of action would be to dismount because it would provide more firepower than just three gunners. Actually, at that point, it would be only two gunners because one of our guys had been knocked unconscious.

"So we got out of our trucks and sprinted to a berm where we could get a clear view of the field, and, like I said, there were several insurgents out there, and we just immediately began returning fire." recalled Sgt. Hester.

Knowing the terrain, the enemy insurgents utilized irrigation ditches and an orchard as concealment for their planned complex attack. The enemy also utilized older civilian cars combat parked along a road perpendicular to the route with all doors and trunks open. The enemy's intent was to destroy the convoy, to inflict maximum casualties, and to kidnap several convoy drivers or US Soldiers.

The start of the ambush disabled and set on fire the lead convoy vehicle, which effectively blocked the southbound lanes, trapping the convoy in the kill zone. The squad leader, Staff

Sergeant Timothy Nein, directed the squad to move forward, traveling on the right shoulder and passing through the engagement area between the enemy and the convoy.

Sgt. Hester directed her gunner to provide heavy volumes of MK-19 grenade launcher and M240B machine gun fire into the field where an overwhelming number of insurgents were executing a well-coordinated ambush on the convoy.

Staff Sergeant Nein ordered the squad to flank the insurgents on their right side. The squad continued to come under heavy machine gun fire and rocket-propelled grenade fire. Sgt. Hester stopped her vehicle at a flanking position, near the orchard field, where over a dozen insurgents were engaging the squad and convoy.

Sgt. Hester directed her gunner to focus fires on the trench line and the orchard field. She then dismounted and moved to what was thought to be the non-contact side of the vehicle.

"We got out of our trucks and ran to a berm where we could get a clear view of the field, and, like I said, there were several insurgents out there, and we just immediately began returning fire." Said Hester.

She ordered her gunner to continue to fire on the orchard field as she and her driver engaged insurgents in the orchard field with small arms. Sergeant Hester began engaging the insurgents with her under barrel-mounted M203 automatic grenade launcher to suppress the heavy incoming enemy fire.

Sgt. Hester followed Staff Sgt. Nein to the right-side berm and threw two well-placed fragmentation grenades into the trench, eliminating several enemy combatants.

Sgt. Hester and Staff Sgt. Nein decided to become offensive by going forward over the berm and into the trench. Once in close-quarters range, they began clearing the enemy enclave with their rifles. Sergeant Hester engaged and eliminated three enemy insurgents to her front with accurate short bursts of fire. They then made their way to the front trench and cleared that as well. After clearing the front trench, a cease-fire was called, and she began securing the ambush site.

The final result of the ambush was twenty-seven enemy fighters killed, six wounded, and one captured. Sgt. Leigh Anne Hester is the first female US Army soldier to receive the Silver Star since World War II and the first ever to be cited for valor in close-quarters combat. She is also the recipient of the Bronze Star and the Army Commendation Medal.

Source:

2014 Hall of Fame Inductees – Army Women's Foundation.

INFOAGE HONORS A HERO | InfoAge Science and History Museums. **https://www.infoage.org/2020/06/24/infoage-honors-a-hero/**

INFOAGE HONORS A HERO | InfoAge Science and History Museums. **https://www.infoage.org/2020/06/24/infoage-honors-a-hero/**

LEIGH HESTER | SCULPTOR JON HAIR. https://www.jonhair.com/copy-2-of-margaret-corbin

Marie Rossi-Cayton

A day after the official ceasefire ended the Gulf War, US Army Chinook helicopter pilot Marie Rossi-Cayton was given a critical mission. Her mission was to fly Iraqi prisoners of war to a drop-off point. Rossi-Cayton and three other US soldiers would tragically pay the ultimate price for that mission.

Marie Rossi was born on January 3, 1959, in Oradell, New Jersey, and grew up in a close-knit Italian-American family. Rossi's first opportunity to serve her country came in college when she joined the Reserve Officers Training Corps. In the 1980s, the US Army firmly maintained the tradition that no women would ever be involved in direct front-line combat. The exclusion law, harking back to World War II, made sure women were kept out of direct combat jobs like the infantry. Only in the late 1970s did the Army accept its first woman pilot for helicopter training.

In 1985, at Camp Humphrey, Korea, Rossi met her future husband, John Cayton, who was a pilot in a Chinook helicopter company. John Cayton recalled that, at the time, he and the other male soldiers questioned her abilities.

"Women were just starting to come into aviation branches at that time, and I was like all the other guys when we heard we were getting our first female, which was Marie.

"Being a part of the boys club, I was just as bad as the rest of them talking trash about having a woman in the unit," Cayton said. "But when she showed up and showed us what she was made of, it changed my mind pretty quick." While it wasn't Rossi's goal to make a career out of the Army, Cayton said that once she found success, she wanted to prove herself.

"We got married in one of the squares in Savannah, Georgia, in fresh blues," he said. "All of my guys in the unit came out, and she wore civilian clothes. She came to the square in a horse and carriage," said Cayton.

Their marriage, however, was soon put on hold as the Iraq army's invasion of Kuwait prompted an immediate build-up of US forces to expel it. They were married just four months when John Cayton deployed with his unit to go over and help draw the line in the sand, so to speak, for President Bush. All the other units back in the States were on alert and getting ready to deploy.

Rossi-Cayton, at that time, was the commander of an air traffic control company at Hunter Army Airfield, but her goal was to get back into flying. When an opening in a Chinook unit became available, the higher-ups promoted Rossi-Cayton to major to allow her to take the job.

"Like all the women that day and time, she had to perform twice as hard as anybody else. That's how she ended up going to the Gulf War as a commander, which was in a combat unit," John Cayton recalled.

Rossi-Cayton and her Chinooks soon arrived in Saudi Arabia. On the eve of the 1991 Gulf War, Major Rossi-Cayton commanded a company of Army CH-47 Chinook helicopters deployed to Saudi Arabia. No American woman had ever flown, let alone led, helicopters into war before, but Rossi-Cayton's Chinooks had orders to fly soldiers and supplies with the 101st Airborne Division into Iraq when the US invasion began.

"Sometimes, you have to disassociate how you feel about the idea of going into war and possibly see the death that is part of the equation. But, as an aviator and a soldier, this is the moment that everybody trains for, and I've worked hard for it, so I feel ready to meet a challenge," Rossi-Cayton stated in an interview.

But as she prepared her crews, which included lower-ranking women pilots and crew chiefs for the invasion, Rossi-Cayton was told she would be pulled away from her unit.

John Cayton added, "The Army tried to pull my wife from her position because she was a woman. She pretty much told them on no uncertain terms, 'You expect me to go back to the States and leave my other two female pilots and my female crew chiefs over here? We got a unit ready to go into combat, and you're going, at the last minute, to pull the commander?' She said, 'No, that ain't gonna happen,'" he recalled. "And it didn't."

On February 24, 1991, Rossi-Cayton led a flight of her company's Chinook helicopters fifty miles deep behind enemy lines into Iraq. Her mission was ferrying essential fuel and ammunition during the first hours of the Coalition Forces' ground assault. Based on her success, her company continued supply missions throughout the war.

Among the first woman to fly in combat and the first to command a unit, Rossi-Cayton took an all-business view of her role. In a widely seen news interview in the days before the ground War, she said on camera, "What I'm doing is no greater or less than the man who is flying next to me or in back of me."

On March 1, 1991, the day after the ceasefire, Rossi-Cayton was tasked with transporting Iraqi prisoners of war. After successfully dropping them off, she led five Chinooks back to base camp as dusk quickly approached.

"They were supposed to be back in plenty of time before dark. They should've been on night vision goggles, but they weren't," John Cayton stated.

As darkness descended, Rossi-Cayton's Chinook slammed into a remote microwave tower. Rossi-Cayton was killed, along with pilot Chief Warrant Officer Robert Hughes, flight engineer Staff Sgt. Mike Garrett, and Crew Chief William Brace.

Brian Miller, an infantryman, was the only soldier to survive the crash. Miller earlier volunteered to be a door gunner and was assigned to Rossi-Cayton's Chinook.

"I have thought about this millions of times. *How? How did I survive?* Because everyone was just mutilated and me coming out with just some broken bones and stuff like that," Miller said.

Later the next day, at a separate military base, John Cayton was called into a hangar. He thought he was about to get "a good chewing out" for something that happened the day before. He saw Rossi-Cayton's brigade commander, battalion commander, and Billy, his best man at their wedding, who was also Rossi's executive officer.

"John, I'm sorry, but that Chinook you heard about that crashed last night that was Marie," Rossi's battalion commander said.

"It was a shotgun to the face. Then I just broke down," John Cayton said. Until then, he had not even heard about any Chinook's crashing.

Major Marie Rossi-Cayton was buried on March 11, 1991, with full military honors at Arlington National Cemetery. In 1992, Rossi-Cayton was inducted into the Army Aviation Hall of Fame. She was the recipient of the Bronze Star, Purple Heart, Air Medal, National Service Defense Medal South West Asia Service Medal w/ Bronze Stars & Army Commendation Medal.

Source:

Marie Therese Rossi - Carry The Load. https://www.carrytheload.org/tribute-wall/marie-therese-rossi/

Daisy Romero

At that very moment, I didn't know if I was alive or not because I thought I was seeing from like a bird's eye view, watching myself. We were on a regular patrol, and I think the blast came from a pressure plate. We were patrolling in Ranger single file; everybody was stepping on it. I had just happened to be two people behind the guy who stepped on the device.

And so the gap between the guy in front of me was a pretty good distance to where all I sustained were some burns. The entire first layer of my eye skin kind of melted off. These eyelashes aren't mine; these eyebrows aren't mine. My hairline suffered.

Thank God I had eye protection; otherwise, I probably would've lost my eyeballs. The guy in front of me got burned on his back, too, and the explosion was so severe that it knocked me back. I remember I was just on my back, thinking that I couldn't get up.

They took me to the closest Forward Operating Base and treated my burns. They kept me there for a couple of days, and I was like, yeah, I'm fine. Really, it's just burns. I just had to put an ointment on my skin and everything, but it sounds more severe than it was. But yeah, that was just another traumatic brain injury [TBI] I suffered while I was out there."

★★★

My name is Daisy Romero, and I am a US Marine. I was born in South Central Los Angeles, and my family moved around a lot due to financial issues. My recruiter at the Marines told me that if I wanted an easy way, I could join a different branch, but this is the toughest branch in the military, so if I wanted a challenge, I had to come to the Marine Corps. Coming from Los Angeles and having a Mexican upbringing, you don't want to be a punk, so I joined the Marines.

After boot camp, I was stationed in Okinawa, Japan. I loved being part of the Marine division, although it came with a lot of challenges because I was always one of one. I was always the first and only Hispanic female Marine.

I was fortunate enough to be surrounded by people who really cared about me. I always talk about my first staff sergeant, who taught me how to be a female Marine, and my staff sergeant was a male. And people are like, what do you mean by that? Well, when you are surrounded by men in that type of environment, you don't know how to act, you don't know what to say, and you don't know if you belong.

And so this staff sergeant said, "Just be yourself. Just know that you will always be one of the very few or one of one, and believe you're going to succeed in every environment you are thrown in." So that's exactly what I did, and I've been doing my entire career, and it's paid out pretty well so far.

I deployed on two combat tours in Afghanistan. I thought I was coming into these deployments as an outcast being a woman. But that wasn't the case. These men took me under their wing and showed me exactly what to do and how to do it. And so I felt very much I was part of the team.

I was part of the Female Engagement Team during my second combat deployment, and it was the same thing. When we arrived, you could sense the guys saying they didn't want females there. They're like, why do we need females to help us do our job? And really, once we helped them understand how to employ us, everybody had bought into us being there. In general, everybody was very welcoming.

The female engagement teams are attached to an infantry company or a line company. We are the ones who deal with the Afghani women we encounter on patrol and gain their trust while respecting their customs.

And so I was with Golf Two Nine, and we supplemented the 5th Marines in Marjah, then Sangin, Afghanistan. At times, it was very difficult. You're out patrolling for twelve-plus klicks a day, and it's physically very demanding. But the harder part is getting close to some of these people, some of these men, and being unable to say goodbye to them sometimes for the last time.

You'd come back from patrol and find out that somebody got killed, and you're like, I was just talking with him this morning. We had just made each other coffee that morning, and now they're gone. And you don't get to say goodbye. You don't get to grieve because then, boom, it's the next morning, and you have to go out on your mission and do it again.

One time, we were maneuvering away from a firefight, and we were just going over these canals that you sometimes have to jump across. Sometimes, they're super huge; sometimes, they're only a foot wide.

But when you have to jump over these canals and run through all this crazy terrain, you're not paying attention to what's coming for you. You're just trying to stay safe and follow your squad leader. You have all this adrenaline running through you as you're running. And so we finally got inside the compound, and I'm just trying to catch my breath.

One of the guys looks at me and says, "What the hell happened to your helmet?" And I'm like, "What do you mean? Is it off? I don't know." And so I take it off, I look at it, and there's a bullet round lodged in the very center of my Kevlar helmet, and I'm like, oh my gosh, I got chills.

It was in the front of the helmet, and I don't remember getting knocked back or feeling a pain in my head. I don't remember any of that. And I'm thinking, well, thank God they have shitty bullets over here.

There were just a lot of times when we had to patrol following each other's footsteps. We didn't want to set off or detonate any hidden bombs, so that was a lot of stress. On one of those patrols, the guy in front of me goes over some terrain, and then I go, and the guy behind me gets blown up.

The guy stepped on the explosive device, and there was nothing really left of him. I remember hearing a loud explosion in my ears, and then all I can remember is from a day or two after the event.

They said after the explosion, they put smelling salts over my nose to see if I could come to, and I immediately woke up. They told me before I passed out that I triaged other people, too. And I was like, I don't remember any of that. They told me I was putting tourniquets on the guy behind me, and then I went out and looked for his missing limbs.

After that, I don't remember the next two days. Apparently, after the explosion, I went on back-to-back patrols. I think I had a bad concussion or TBI. So, I think my ability to continue and just be on autopilot is amazing because I have no recollection of those following two days, but I was still fully functioning.

I often questioned why did I survive? I got within two feet of the explosive device; why was I spared? But I knew I had to reel myself back in and realize it just wasn't my time. And there's a purpose for everything. And I think the reason why a lot of us are so open about telling our stories is so that we keep our friend's memories alive, or else we'll be doing them a disservice. What did they die for?

There were several other harrowing incidents. On one of my first deployments, I was operating in a mounted convoy. In my truck, there was the driver, myself, the gunner, and we had an interpreter. We warned the interpreter to be really careful when he gets out of the vehicle.

We had been on this convoy for about five or six hours, and for whatever reason, the interpreter couldn't pee in the bottle we gave him, so he held it for a long time. After about five hours, the convoy came to a stop. I cracked my door open, and suddenly, I heard a big booming explosion.

I didn't know if something hit us or if it was a rocket-propelled grenade. I was very disoriented. I wasn't knocked unconscious, but I didn't know where I was... I was very confused. I started calling out the names of my guys to check on them. Then, we called for the interpreter to check on him.

I got out of my side and walked over to where he was in the back, and literally, the entire back of our vehicle was blown apart. So I started looking around. I could see his leg dangling out this bent door. I yanked open the damaged door, and the entire front part of his body was gone.

I don't know what came over me, but I just lost it and started telling him, "We fucking told you to wait for us before getting out; you could have killed more Marines." And I'm sitting here talking to this dead guy, and at that point, my friends knew. They're like, "Oh, yeah, she's fucked up, we need to pull her out." They sat me down, I think, in the armadillo truck that was following us, and they told me to stay in there.

The Doc eventually came back there, and he tells me, "Yeah, you have a TBI." But my thing was, I always stayed shut and didn't tell them about my injuries because I didn't want to get pulled out of the fight. I didn't want them to be down one person. I didn't want them to be like, oh, we need this many Marines to go out, and now we can't conduct our mission because we don't have enough people. I didn't want to diminish our capabilities. So yeah, I always kept my mouth shut.

Coming back from war was the hardest part. I wanted to get back out there on patrol. I wanted to be with my team. I tried so many times to go back.

—Daisy Romero

★ ★ ★

Source:

Monica Lin Brown

The gunner shouted, "Shut the door," as the deadly hail of incoming machine-gun fire started raking and pinging off the Humvee. They were trapped... caught in an insurgent enemy ambush. As the .50 caliber machine gunner started pouring suppressive fire back at the enemy, Staff Sergeant Santos turned to combat medic Specialist Brown and yelled, "Let's go, Doc."

Monica Brown, a girl from a small town, beat the odds by becoming a US Army paratrooper and a Silver Star recipient. The first women to actually receive the Silver Star were four World War II Army nurses.

Monica Brown's Silver Star came at a time when the Pentagon policy prohibited women from serving in front-line combat roles in the infantry, armor, or artillery. But the nature of the wars in Afghanistan and Iraq, with no actual front lines, allowed women soldiers to take part in close-quarters combat more so than in any other previous conflicts.

Growing up in a small Texas town, Monica excelled in sports, running track and cross country in high school. "Running is like meditation for me; I can just think without anyone talking to me," said Monica.

Early on, Monica became interested in radiology through an aunt who was an X-ray technician. She found it engrossing enough to consider it as a future career. Later, an Army recruiter informed her that she could receive radiology training in the military, and they would pay for it.

A few months later, she disappointingly learned that the Army radiology program was canceled, so she enlisted in the Army as a Healthcare Specialist, which is a fancy way to say she was a combat medic.

During Basic and Advanced Individual Training, Monica met her mentor, a drill sergeant whose impact would help define who she would become in the Army. "She was high-speed and airborne-qualified."

Her independence and strong personality set her apart. "I wanted to be high-speed like that. My drill instructor was from the 82nd Airborne Division and had that maroon beret and the Airborne patch. I knew I wanted to be like her," recalled Monica.

After completing Airborne School, Monica was assigned to the Forward Support Company of the 82nd Airborne Division. On February 7, 2007, Private First Class Brown deployed to Afghanistan to Forward Operating Base Salerno.

At first, Monica was kept working strictly on the base. "The first actual patient I worked on was an Afghani man who had a gunshot to his leg. My reaction was, 'My gosh, this is a real person, and these are real injuries; this isn't training anymore.' That's when the switch flipped, and I think everything changed from training to me really liking my job," said Monica.

In March 2007, a small outpost occupied by the 73rd Cavalry requested a female medic, and Monica was chosen. The outpost was little more than a cluster of tents with no plumbing or running water. The perimeter was surrounded and protected by dirt-filled walls.

Monica's aid station was a tiny 8-by-5-foot area barely big enough to fit a stretcher. "I loved it and the challenge," she said. She went on some resupply and humanitarian missions with Delta Troop.

To respect Afghani traditions, any medical treatment of an Afghan woman had to be conducted by a woman. Women throughout the country were also excluded from basic medical treatment facilities by the Taliban unless the facility exclusively treated women.

The Outpost Charlie Troop was running combat patrol, and in April, their other medic went on leave. US Military regulations stipulated that women weren't supposed to be assigned to any front-line units. Still, Monica was the only medic available, and she received orders to accompany the patrol.

When Monica arrived, Charlie Troop received orders to go on a search-and-capture mission. They would be out in enemy territory for five nights. The patrol consisted of four heavily armored Humvees and one Afghan National Army pickup truck.

Having spent the night just outside the small village of Jani Khel, Charlie Troop was informed on the morning of April 25, 2007, that two Taliban insurgents lived in the town. They spent the day searching the small village and found nothing; the enemy had already fled the area.

By late afternoon, they started moving out of the village, one by one, turning off the road into a dry riverbed adjacent to it. Monica rode in the Humvee with the platoon sergeant, Staff Sergeant Jose Santos. She never heard the explosion, but the .50 caliber gunner on her Humvee yelled, "Two ones hit. I see smoke and a tire rolling through the field."

The rear Humvee, with five soldiers inside, had driven over an improvised explosive device (IED) that utilized a pressure plate for detonation. Looking back, they saw the Humvee engulfed in a fireball, and its fuel tank and reserve fuel cans ignited. Monica instinctively grabbed her medical bag and her weapon and opened the door.

The .50 caliber gunner yelled down, "Shut the door," as incoming machine-gun fire started hitting the Humvee. They were trapped in a classic ambush. The .50 caliber gunner immediately turned around and began laying a heavy stream of suppressive fire toward the enemy. Staff Sgt. Santos turned to Monica and shouted, "Let's go, Doc."

With Staff Sgt. Santos a couple of steps ahead of her, they ran approximately three hundred yards through the heavy silt blanketing the dry river bed. Enemy machine-gun and rifle fire chased them as they sprinted to their objective, the burning Humvee.

Four of the injured had been thrown from the vehicle; the fifth, Specialist Larry Spray, was caught inside by his boot and was on fire. Sergeant Zachary Tellier, without hesitation, entered the burning truck and managed to pull him out.

Out of breath and with her heart racing from the riverbed sprint, Monica observed that all five of the soldiers were injured. Some appeared to be going into shock, stumbling, and disoriented, while others suffered from burns and profuse bleeding caused by numerous cuts and abrasions.

Specialists Stanson Smith and Larry Spray were in critical condition. Spray had severe burns, and Smith had a severe laceration on his forehead, blinding him in a mask of his own blood.

Monica and one of the lesser injured soldiers grabbed Smith by his body armor and dragged him into the safety of a ditch fifteen yards away. Sergeant Tellier quickly assisted Spray to the ditch.

"I did not really think about anything except for getting the guys to a safer location and getting them taken care of," Monica recalled. The other vehicles from the convoy turned around to form a crescent formation and began to return heavy fire at numerous enemy positions.

The enemy spotted the hapless soldiers hunkering down in the ditch and started dropping mortar rounds towards them. Monica threw her body over Smith, shielding him, and yelled to another soldier to cover up the other casualty as more than a dozen rounds landed around them, kicking dirt and debris into the air, adding to the chaos.

Just then if the situation couldn't get any worse, the ammunition cache inside the burning Humvee started to cook off and explode: 60mm mortars, 40mm grenade rounds, and rifle ammunition going off in all directions. Again, Monica threw herself over the wounded to shield them with her body.

Lieutenant Robbins, the platoon leader, moved his Humvee near the injured and was amazed that Monica had survived. Robbins later stated, "I was surprised I didn't get killed in those exposed few minutes I was out there and Pfc. Brown had been out there for at least ten to fifteen minutes or longer.

"There was small arms fire coming in from two different machine-gun positions, mortars falling, a burning Humvee with sixteen mortar rounds in it, and chunks of aluminum the size of softballs flying all around. It was about as hairy as it gets."

Staff Sgt. Santos drove the Afghan pickup truck over to get the wounded; he would later recall that bullets were impacting within inches of Pfc. Brown, but she steadfastly remained focused on treating the casualties. Lieutenant Robbins also commented on her calm demeanor under fire, "Pfc. Brown was focused on her patients the whole time. She did her job perfectly."

Monica and Staff Sgt. Santos pulled Smith onto the truck while Larry Spray crouched behind the back window. Once the truck started moving, Monica dove over the front seat onto a bench in the back. She continued to work by putting pressure on the heavily bleeding laceration on Smith's head. She held Spray's hand, giving him comfort, as his charred body started to shake. She continued asking Spray questions to prevent him from going into shock.

Staff Sgt. Santos drove across the river and stopped behind one of the Humvees; Monica set up her Casualty Collection Point there. Smith was bleeding heavily and slipping in and out of consciousness, and Spray had extensive burns.

Monica bandaged Smith, then started IVs on both soldiers. She expertly covered Spray's burns with gauze and put him in a hypothermia bag. She soon had them stabilized and prepped for medevac, but it was another forty-five minutes before the helicopters arrived.

Monica recalled, "When the medevac helicopter was taking off, and everything was quiet, my ears were still ringing. I couldn't hear anything. I was walking through the field back to the Humvees, through shin-high green grass, blowing because the bird was taking off. I remember thinking, 'Did that just really happen? Did I do everything right?' When I got back to the trucks the guys were all hugging me and thanking me."

Staff Sergeant Aaron Best, who served as Lieutenant Robbin's .50 caliber gunner that day, said, "I've seen a lot of grown men who didn't have the courage and weren't able to handle themselves under fire like Monica did. She never missed a beat."

Two days later, her superiors abruptly pulled Monica from the field. She had attracted too much attention. Specialists Smith and Spray were flown back to the US and eventually recovered from their wounds.

On March 21st, 2008, the US Army flew Monica's brother Justin to Bagram Airbase to stand beside her as Vice President Dick Cheney presented nineteen-year-old Combat Medic, Army Specialist Monica Lin Brown the Silver Star.

The military said Monica Brown's "bravery, unselfish actions and medical aid rendered under fire saved the lives of her comrades and represents the finest traditions of heroism in combat."

Monica said she never expected to be in a situation like that and credits her training and instructors for her actions that day. She added, "I realized that everything I had done during the attack was just from repetitive memory."

Source:

The Belle Banner, Belle Missouri February 21st 2018

03/21/2008 dvids CBS interview

History, Life in the Army John Stockton November 7, 2018

Monica Brown | What Life in the Army is really like.. https://lifeinthearmy.com/2018/11/07/monica-brown/

(2022). Memorial Day salute. Columbian, (), A.1.

Jorge L Pena-Romero - OurWarHeroes.org - Tribute sites by Q Madp. http://www.iraqwarheroes.org/penaromero.htm

Female Texas Teen To Receive Silver Star - CBS News. https://www.cbsnews.com/news/female-texas-teen-to-receive-silver-star/

Tammie Jo Shults

It started as an ordinary day, with the steady hum of the engines providing a comforting backdrop as we soared from LaGuardia toward Dallas. An ear-splitting explosion suddenly shattered the calm, a violent unknown force slamming into the Captain's side of the plane like a Mack truck crashing into a cement wall. The aircraft lurched, veering dangerously as it snapped into a roll, the world outside twisting into a blur.

For a fleeting moment, we attempted to focus on our instrument panel; however, the chaotic, violent dance of the plane mixed with the frantic flashing lights blurred our vision.

In normal situations, you hit turbulence, and then it subsides, but this time, it didn't; it just crescendoed as the nightmare was just starting to unfold. And then there was a noise that wasn't just loud; it simply smothered everything. We couldn't hear each other, we couldn't hear our own voices, and an ice pick of pain slowly dug deeper into our ears.

Time seemed to stretch as we fought for control, smoke filling the cockpit as the plane plummeted toward oblivion. Hearts racing, we fought the controls with white-knuckled intensity, desperately trying to coax the wounded aircraft back to stability. Every second felt like an eternity as we were acutely aware of the fragile thread that held our fate in the sky...

Tammie Jo Shults is known for being one of the first female fighter pilots to serve in the US Navy. She proudly served during the Iraq War in Operation Desert Storm. Shults was born on November 2, 1961, and grew up on a ranch in southern New Mexico. She first learned about fighter pilots on the ranch.

★ ★ ★

The jets from Holman Air Force Base would anchor their dogfighting maneuvers over our big hay barn. Later, I found out that you need a visual reference point on the ground to do your dogfighting, so our big barn was the last thing on the road there in Tularosa. As I watched them practicing maneuvers, I was usually mucking out stalls or stock trailers of organic fertilizer, and it just looked like a lot of fun.

We even had a sonic boom one night that spooked our cattle. When we woke up the next morning, there was just an empty corral. It had spooked them, and they had laid down a fence post on one side of the corral, and Dad didn't complain. He just said, 'Go get your horses, follow the tracks.' And we found them all about a mile away. But I laugh now also in knowing that truly, at 10,000 feet doing dog fighting, we should not have been having sonic booms on our ranch. I think there was a little bit of freelance flying going on at the time.

I was drawn to military aviation and grew up in a very patriotic family. My dad served during the Korean War, and I thought the military could be a great opportunity for me. I really hadn't any idea of how a woman could serve in the military. When I saw the fighter jets streaking across the sky, I put the two ideas together, and I thought this was my cup of tea.

I started reading books about pilots and airplanes and came across my first aviation hero, Nate Saint, in the book, Jungle Pilot. Saint had his start in the military for no money down, which was what I had, and I just started seeing a faint footpath for myself from barnyard to cockpit.

Growing up working on the ranch definitely led to my work ethic. Also, growing up with a dad and brothers who treated me as an equal, they expected the same thing from me: no excuses.

The Navy wasn't my first choice, but I look at that now, and I couldn't be more thankful for all the no's I received along the way. Because the Navy was ahead of its time as far as women were concerned, women in the Navy were allowed to fly tactical aircraft and tactical missions before the combat exclusion policy was lifted.

I would have to say Officer Candidate School was as fair as could be at that point in the Navy; women had their heads shaved like everybody else; we had no special treatment at all and did push-ups and physical training like everybody else.

And I went there prepared physically; I can't say I knocked the academics out of the house at all. I'd never even spelled the word aerodynamics before I got there. So, there was a lot of learning to be done.

The Military's Combat Exclusion Policy prevented women from flying combat sorties. Our squadron studied Chinese, Russian, and French weapons and tactics and then simulated those against our own fleet from top gun students, other squadrons, single ships, and entire carrier groups.

Shults and her team provided invaluable electronic warfare training to Navy ships and aircraft. Her persistence in breaking barriers finally paid off as she became one of the first women to fly the F/A-18 Hornet fighter jet in a support role. After ten years of service, Shults achieved the rank of Navy lieutenant commander. In 1993, she retired from the US Navy and began flying for commercial airlines.

On April 17, 2018, Shults was working for Southwest Airlines as a Captain, commanding Flight 1380 from New York to Dallas, when a life-threatening event occurred.

At approximately 11 a.m., cruising at an altitude of 32,500 feet, the airplane suffered a catastrophic engine failure. One of the turbine fan blades in the left engine suddenly broke, shredding the engine and hurling shrapnel into the left wing and tail, causing further damage.

The loss of all power in the left engine pushed the plane into a hard left roll and dive. The explosion was so violent that it severed several hydraulic lines and a fuel line and blew out a passenger window in row fourteen, resulting in explosive decompression.

Simultaneously, the cockpit filled with thick haze, making it impossible for Tammie Jo and Copilot First Officer Darren Ellisor to see. To make matters worse, the plane shook so violently that they could barely read the instruments even after the haze cleared.

One passenger, Jennifer Riordan, was partially sucked through the damaged window and tragically was later pronounced dead at the hospital. Captain Shults made an emergency descent and landed successfully in Philadelphia.

Southwest Airlines officials and passengers noted Shults' actions, calm demeanor, and competence during the emergency. Shults later revealed that she had not intended to be the pilot of that flight but had swapped the shift with her husband.

Shults in an interview with reporter Jeff Simon Shults recalled the events:

Well, it was a normal day, and we were on our second leg, leaving LaGuardia for Dallas. We heard an explosion, and it felt like a Mack truck had T-boned us on the Captain's side of the plane.

It was a pretty hard hit. The fire extinguisher came off the wall, and all the oxygen masks were flying around, so it was a forceful impact. The aircraft suddenly just tucked over and did a snap roll to the left, and then we caught it.

We could see the engine instruments for a moment when the explosion happened. The engine instruments were flashing and rolling, and then snap the plane dove. We caught it and were very careful about bringing the plane back. We balanced our flight with our rudder after losing the engine.

In normal situations, you hit turbulence, and then it subsides or something to that effect, and this didn't; it just crescendoed. Then, there was a noise that wasn't just loud; it simply smothered out everything else. We couldn't hear each other, and the shuttering kept us from being able to focus our eyes on our instruments or our checklists for a little while.

We slowly brought the nose of the plane up. We both had this ice-pick pain stabbing into our ears, and we were having trouble breathing. We had to put on our oxygen masks one at a time, so there was always somebody with their hands on the controls, the yolk.

Even before we could communicate, we used sign language and tapped each other on the shoulder to get attention. Initially, we actually had a lot of smoke in the cockpit. I think that was brought in from the explosion through the AC system, and then that intensified a bit with the condensation that was formed whenever the fan blade had sheared. It actually helixed forward in the engine compartment and caused a sonic boom.

It blew the rim of the engine right off into two pieces. Air Traffic Control said it was a large enough piece of debris that they tracked it to the ground, but the smaller pieces were the ones that really did the damage. They're the ones that the cowling peeled back a little bit like a banana peel, and then the smaller pieces of debris took out chunks of the wing.

The debris severed hydraulic and fuel lines on that side of the plane. One of the passenger windows got hit by one of those big buckles underneath the engine that locks down the cowling. It was a hard enough impact that the window gave way, and that's where our rapid depressurization came from.

A later released Air Traffic recording revealed Captain Shults advising: "Southwest 1380, we're single engine, we have part of the aircraft missing, so we're going to need to slow down a bit. We are requesting medical personnel to meet us on the runway. We've got injured passengers."

Air Traffic Control responded, "Injured passengers, OK, and is your airplane physically on fire?"

"No, it's not on fire, but part of it's missing. They said there's a hole, and, uh, we think someone went out," Shults responded.

Amid the calamity, passengers on Flight 1380 used their phones to text loved ones and share news of their desperate state. Passenger Marty Martinez wrote in the caption of a livestream video, showing himself breathing through a mask, "Something is wrong with our plane! It appears we are going down!"

Shults added: "I have to give such credit to my crew. My co-pilot, Darren Ellisor, was my first officer that day. Amazing man. Under pressure, I have to say, having a great team means a lot when you're dealing with so much and in a combination that's never been taught before, never been experienced. Our flight attendants also all performed above and beyond in their duties that day.

★★★

When we got our oxygen masks on, we knew that we were able to control the aircraft because we were able to get the shuttering to the point where we could finally read our instruments. From there, we were able to get ahold of the knobs and switches that we needed.

Having smelled the smoke, I shut the fuel shut off and secured the engine from further damage. Darren and I agreed on landing in Philadelphia and started to head that way. I just thought a lot about the people in the back, the way a lot of commercial pilots feel about their customers.

As startling as it was for Darren and me, I'm sure it was mind-numbing for those passengers in the back. So, I made a quick announcement. It wasn't eloquent by any means. I just said, 'This is your captain speaking; we're not going down. We're going into Philly.'

We descended maybe close to 19–20,000 feet in the first five minutes, which isn't extraordinary. It's definitely steeper than what we planned, but we had a lot of drag helping us get down. And then, when we got closer to Philadelphia, they asked us to level off at 4,000 feet going across the city.

We assumed that we could pull it off, and whenever we pulled the nose up to level off, the airspeed just continued to vacuum off. There was a certain controllability issue with too much thrust. We only had enough rudder authority for so much thrust from the working engine because of all the drag. When you have that much drag pulling you left, and you add power on the right, then airplanes don't fly well sideways.

So we were trying to keep away from being on the backside of that lift drag ratio, and I also could see our wing chewed up with damage. I had been flying for quite some time just because it was protocol and procedure that the Captain does the emergency landing.

Darren had done a great job. He was the one that was initially flying, and when we got hit with that fan blade explosion, we both grabbed it, and then we divided up duties, and he flew for a little while, while I took care of public announcement and finding a runway and things like that. We did a number of things differently that day, but having the training, the systems, and the checklist created a mental flow.

When you can't read your checklist, or there's a lot of chatter that you're answering or dealing with in an emergency, it becomes way more challenging. So, sometimes, you just have to get creative. I know in the final section of our approach, there was so much chaos and chatter that I just pointed to the flap inhibit switch, and Darren flipped it. So, being creative and communicative, we both had ideas but would defer to the other person's idea if it was better. There's no pride in that cockpit.

I asked Traffic Control for the closest suitable field because we were shuttering so much that I really couldn't figure it out.

Darren had his map already out and advised me to try to get to Philadelphia. So, I gave up my plan and followed his.

I can't say enough about how well flight attendants performed in the back. They were dealing with a whole different world than we were. And when they heard the announcement that we had a destination, they unbuckled their safety belts and went down the aisles in a very rough ride. By procedure and protocol, they could have stayed buckled up, but they changed the ending of that day by acting compassionately and getting up and helping people.

We had a young mom with a six-month-old traveling by herself. She could not wrestle the oxygen mask and the baby and all this. We had passengers, Andrew Needham, Tim McGinty, Peggy Phillips, that got up and faced that same adversity and went towards a very dangerous broken window to help people.

It's also amazing the impact of even that one sentence we managed to get over the PA. That information of telling the passengers that we're not going down and that we're going to land in Philadelphia made a huge difference. I think we forget how powerful communication is. It doesn't have to be eloquent to be useful. And when we give people a little bit of information, that definitely can trigger hope. That hope did not change our circumstances for the next twenty minutes, but it did change us and how we acted.

★★★

The damaged airliner was still able to touch down on its landing gear. As it traveled down the runway, the airport tower told the plane's flight crew members to turn right and stop wherever they could.

"Thank you. We're going to stop right here by the fire trucks. Thanks, guys, for the help." Shults casually told the air traffic controller.

The plane landed safely, and the stunned passengers were amazed to have made it to the ground. As medics filled the plane,

Shults entered the cabin to talk to each of the passengers, shake their hands, and comfort them.

Benjamin Goldstein, who was traveling on that flight, shared his memory of the event when Shults walked back into the cabin, "I asked her, 'Do I get a hug too?' and she smiled and told me, 'Of course. I wouldn't let you by without a hug.' It was very touching. Here at the most crucial moment, she had the presence of mind and the courage to act with excellence as it was required. It's a beautiful quality, and we have our lives to thank for it," said Goldstein.

Alfred Tumlinson who was traveling with his wife, was amazed by Shults' calmness and stated, "She has nerves of steel."

The National Transportation Safety Board sent investigators the next morning to determine the cause of engine failure. They found out that parts of the protective engine housing had broken off mid-flight and were recovered in Berks County, Pennsylvania, roughly seventy miles northwest of Philadelphia International Airport, where the plane eventually landed.

Southwest Airlines issued a statement the day after the event, acknowledging the efforts of pilot Shults and first officer Darren Ellisor. Both Shults and Ellisor avoided media interviews at the time and gave a joint statement. They were empathetic to the family of Jennifer Riordan, who was killed aboard the flight, the one casualty of the engine explosion.

"As Captain and First Officer of the crew of five who worked to serve our customers aboard flight 1380 yesterday, we all feel we were simply doing our jobs," the airline reported in the statement. "Our hearts are heavy. On behalf of the entire crew, we appreciate the outpouring of support from the public and our coworkers as we all reflect on one family's profound loss."

To learn more about Tammie Jo Shults please check out her book, *Nerves of Steel.*

Source:

Social Flight Live interview with Jeff Simon

Smithsonian National Air and Space Museum interview "Adventure is worthwhile": Tammie Jo Shults (Earhart Lecture)

Nerves of Steel - Today's Christian Living. https://todayschristianliving.org/nerves-of-steel/

Tammi Jo Shults. https://www.hillvets.org/team-36/tammi-jo-shults

https://www.dallasnews.com/business/2018/04/18/after-landing-troubled-southwest-plane-pilot-tammie-jo-shults-hugged-passengers-texted-god-is-good/

Danielle Green

It was 2004, and we were operating in Central Baghdad when I got hit. I went up to the rooftop to help provide security to my team, and two rocket-propelled grenades hit a barricade below. I remember something whizzing by me and landing two stories below, almost hitting our parked Humvees.

I grabbed my weapon, and the next incoming RPG hit me. I was knocked down and lying on my side, and my first thoughts were of anger. I was angry that I was gonna die in this awful country.

After a successful career playing basketball at Notre Dame, Danielle Green, at twenty-five years old, enlisted in the US Army. She was motivated by a desire to serve her country and give back. As a military police officer, Green was deployed to Iraq in 2004, where the danger was constantly present. During a routine rooftop security mission, her life was irrevocably changed by an ambush.

★ ★ ★

At some point after I was hit on that rooftop, I realized I wasn't going to die, and that's when I remember saying a prayer. My prayer was if I survived, I wanted to have a child, and believe it or not, I felt a surge of energy hit my body. But even with that surge, I was still too weak to get up. I looked down at my tattered uniform, and it was covered in blood. I mean, there was blood everywhere.

I heard a voice in the distance shout, 'Green, are you OK?' I could move only my neck and head; the helmet was making it even more difficult. I heard the footsteps of my Sergeant begin making his way up the stairs, and I replied, 'Sarge, I'm hurt!'

I still remember the green-blue of his eyes and the look of horror on his face when he finally saw me. But at that point, I still didn't know I was missing my arm. I can't imagine what he sees. My sergeant called for more soldiers. One applied a tourniquet to my arm, another to my leg. They grabbed my other limbs to carry me, and I remember repeatedly telling them I was thirsty.

I was taken by helicopter to a Green Zone hospital, and a few hours later, I awoke surrounded by my comrades; they all had tears in their eyes. I couldn't figure out why they were all crying and said, 'You all look like somebody just died—I'm alive.' That was the first time I looked down... I say, 'Hey, is my arm missing; is it gone?' And one of my battle buddies says, 'Yeah, bud, you lost your arm.

I cried for maybe a few seconds, and I got myself together. A battalion commander came in and awarded me with a purple heart, and each of my fellow soldiers came forward and kissed me.

One of her combat buddies then came over with the wedding ring that had adorned Green's left ring finger. That ring was given to her only seven weeks earlier and was now placed on her right hand. Green's Sergeant had defied orders to evacuate the area immediately and instead stayed, dug through a foot of sand on the rooftop, finding her arm and retrieving it.

"Someone gave me a watch, wished me 'Safe travels,' and I was taken to a military hospital in Germany," Green added.

Green confronted a new reality: she could no longer be the athlete she once was. Medically retired just months later, she began a difficult journey to redefine her identity. Refusing to let her injuries determine her path, she adapted, saying, "It was all challenging. I had to learn everything left-handed, but I had to keep pushing forward."

Green had to deal with her own "why me?" issues. "I lost an arm. I saw a lot of people at Walter Reed Hospital who were much worse off than I am. There's no self-pity here. God could have taken me, but he gave me a little more time to live and fulfill the mission," Green said.

Recognized for her selfless service and determination, she was the recipient of the famed Pat Tillman Award. Tillman was an NFL football legend and US Army Ranger. Tillman walked away from a successful NFL career to serve his country after September 11th. Tillman was killed in Afghanistan on April 22, 2004, in the Khost province.

Danielle Green's spirit shines through her work as a counselor with Veterans Affairs, where she is dedicated to supporting fellow veterans. Green symbolizes hope and resilience, ensuring that her story and those of countless other veterans are never forgotten.

Source:

The man upstairs always has a plan'.
https://www.ndinsider.com/story/sports/womens-basketball/2014/05/26/he-man-upstairs-always-has-a-pla/116986354/

Lori Hill

The last time retired US Army Chief Warrant Officer 3 Lori L. Hill flew a helicopter was when she served during the Iraq War. On one fateful mission, she sustained a gunshot wound when her helicopter was taking heavy incoming enemy fire. The damage forced her to make a dangerous emergency landing. Hill became the first woman awarded the Distinguished Flying Cross for heroism.

Hill says that growing up, she was a shy 17-year-old teenager from Springfield, Oregon, who joined the service to get money for college. She became an OH-58D Kiowa Warrior helicopter pilot in the Air Cavalry and an aviation safety officer.

The Bell OH-58 Kiowa is a smaller family of single-engine, single-rotor military helicopters used for observation, utility, and direct fire support. In Iraq, the Kiowas routinely flew seventy-two hours per month.

In March 2006, during the Iraq War, Hill was conducting a routine reconnaissance flight in her Kiowa helicopter when she and her co-pilot were asked to assist a ground unit being fired upon. Hill's helicopter was hit while trying to suppress the enemy fire and lost hydraulic power. She was left struggling to control and land the helicopter.

Army records about the incident state that Hill drew fire away from the lead helicopter while providing suppressive fire for the ground troops below. A rocket-propelled grenade struck and damaged her helicopter. Despite the complications to the helicopters and flight maneuverability, Hill refused to leave the US troops on the ground and continued until they reached safety.

"You could just hear the bullets pinging and firing off the helicopter, I didn't even know I got shot. I just felt some pain but kept going,' said Hill, recalling that day.

After getting shot in one of her ankles, Hill piloted her damaged aircraft back to the forward operating base, saving her crew and aircraft. Hill says she didn't even realize she had been shot in the ankle until she had landed and sat down to take off her boot.

"I didn't know I was shot until I landed and took off my boot to see what was bothering me. The bullet went through my heel and up my ankle. I was actually glad I didn't pass out while flying. I was relieved to be able to help the ground soldiers out and get our helicopter down safely at the base," said Hill.

Hill was in a cast for six months as her shattered leg bones healed.

Hill's actions led to her becoming one of the few military women awarded the Distinguished Flying Cross (DFC) for heroism. She is also a Purple Heart recipient.

"The hardest thing about learning to fly a helicopter is hovering, but it is like riding a bike. Once you get it, it seems so easy. And I would not be the person I am today if I had not spent those twenty years in the Army. I really loved flying and serving my country. I honestly believe a woman can do any job she wants to, but she has to meet the same standards males do," Hill stated.

Hill's military career shows her serving in Germany, Korea, and Iraq with deployments to Desert Shield/Storm and Operation Iraqi Freedom. Currently, Hill works as a substitute teacher, volunteering at her children's school and pursuing a master's degree in elementary education.

"Women can not only be in the military, but they can do in the military whatever they set their minds to do." —Lori Hill

Source:

Super Heroine - Lift Magazine. https://lift.erau.edu/super-heroine/

6 Women Who Fought In Direct Combat In Iraq And Afghanistan - Task & Purpose. https://taskandpurpose.com/history/6-women-who-fought-in-direct-combat-in-iraq-and-afghanistan/?amp"

6 Women Who Fought In Direct Combat In Iraq And Afghanistan - Task & Purpose. https://taskandpurpose.com/history/6-women-who-fought-in-direct-combat-in-iraq-and-afghanistan/

Does the Army still use the Kiowa? – Turningtooneanother.net. https://turningtooneanother.net/2019/08/15/does-the-army-still-use-the-kiowa/

Liz McConaghy

As the giant tandem-rotor Chinook helicopter ascended into the sky, suddenly, all hell broke loose. The Chinook shook with a loud explosion, and crewman Liz McConaghy was slammed into the side of the metal fuselage.

The pilot fought the controls to stabilize the bucking helicopter before shouting a warning to the crew, "I can't see!" The pilot was blinded by shattered glass fragments from the cockpit window. Confusion reigned. Were they hit by a rocket-propelled grenade? Was it a catastrophic engine failure? Or something much worse?

Liz McConaghy was raised in a small Northern Irish town. Growing up, McConaghy always knew she wanted a career where she could help people. One day, she saw a magazine with a photo on the cover of a soldier hanging out of a helicopter. "Instantly, I wanted to become that. I didn't understand what that was, but I wanted to be it" McConaghy recalled. On her nineteenth birthday, only one week after September 11, 2001, McConaghy joined the Royal Air Force.

Later that year, McConaghy was accepted for aircrew training in the RAF. After two years of training, she qualified as a Chinook crewman and joined Twenty-Seven Squadron. The Twenty-Seven then deployed to Basra, Iraq. At only twenty-one years old, McConaghy became the youngest aircrew to serve during the Iraq

War. She was also the only female crew member of a prestigious Chinook helicopter team.

In 2005, McConaghy received orders for deployment to Afghanistan. There, she would complete ten grueling and dangerous tours as part of the medical emergency helicopter response team, assisting wounded soldiers.

The response team was a challenge McConaghy relished, but the horrors of War would quickly start to add up. The compounding tragedies she would see day and day out would have a devastating impact later on her mental health.

One of four RAF crewmen, part of McConaghy's job was operating one of the two M134 mini-guns mounted to the side of the Chinook, which could fire fifty deadly rounds a second. She also could utilize the M60 machine gun, which could fire 7.62mm caliber ammo at one hundred rounds per minute.

McConaghy, added this in an interview:

These weapons of mass destruction gave us the ability to protect the Chinook from all directions, sometimes without needing to fire a bullet, the sight of them being enough of a deterrent to the enemy. When you pressed the trigger, within seconds, everything you aimed at turned to mush. My other responsibilities were loading and restraining cargo, managing troops, operating sensors, and communications.

Our missions would start when the "bat phone" would ring. We'd take down all the details, sprint out to the aircraft, and spin the aircraft up as quick as we could; engineers would be helping, and most of the time, we'd get very minimal information to begin.

I quickly learned that the injuries in Afghanistan don't just happen by accident. It's usually troops in contact, or there's been an improvised explosive device of some form, so, you know, most of the time, you're kind of going into somewhere that's pretty tasty when you're going to land.

At first, I had this lovely naivety because I was so young. We would think nothing of going into a hail of bullets to get a casualty. It was just picking up everybody's sons, husbands, and dads, who had paid the ultimate price. It was the accumulative effect of that. We saw it all.

★ ★ ★

McConaghy had one of her closest calls in January, 2007, in the Helmand province of Afghanistan. That day, the mission called for two RAF Chinooks to deliver urgent ammunition and supplies to the British Army's forward operating base at Kajaki Dam.

The mission would call for the Chinooks to fly over hostile terrain where past US and British helicopters had been ambushed and shot down. At the time, this area was one of the deadliest War zones in the world, teaming with battle-hardened Taliban insurgents.

McConaghy was on board one of the Chinooks, manning her M60. As the two Chinooks approached the first drop-off point, one helicopter flew security by circling above the area while McConaghy's Chinook descended with its cargo net full of ammo toward the ground, kicking up a large cloud of sand.

As McConaghy's Chinook lifted back into the sky, all hell broke loose. Following a loud bang, McConaghy felt the Chinook shudder and was immediately thrown into the side of the metal fuselage. The pilot shouted, "I can't see!" as he was blinded by splinters of shattered glass from the cockpit. McConaghy, horrified, watched one of her crewmates plunge towards the open central hatch. The crew member was luckily saved by a safety harness.

When McConaghy spotted a large, sparking cable striking the airframe and smelled the burned electricity, she realized they had flown directly into one of those high-voltage wires helicopter crews named "helicopter killers."

"I knew we were about to crash, so I braced myself hard against the door frame and placed my hand on the release straps of my harness," McConaghy recalled.

Just a dozen feet before crashing, the co-pilot regained control of the shuddering Chinook and soared into the sky. The crew had barely escaped a crash landing, which most likely would have killed them all.

The missions in Afghanistan tested the Chinook crew's mental and physical stamina. There were times when they'd fly up to sixteen hours a day. At any time, day or night, the crews were in the air only minutes after receiving orders, and the operations were always different.

One day, they might be delivering tons of ammo and supplies, while on other days, they might be collecting and dropping off troops in dangerous fast-response raids behind enemy lines. As the war grew in intensity, Chinook crews' contact with the enemy increased and constantly came under deadly fire.

"The aircraft rotor noise is so loud that at first you don't hear it. The first thing you notice is the dust being kicked up off the ground surrounding the aircraft as the bullets get closer, then the distinctive 'ting, ting, ting' as they begin to hit the metal of the aircraft frame. Because it's so hard to identify a firing point where the rounds are coming from, you just have to stand your ground at the mini-gun and pray that there's a little protective glow surrounding you."

On her busiest day of operations in 2008, she and her crew flew fourteen separate sorties, including one operation where five British soldiers had been killed at a forward operating base.

"We flew in and landed to collect our fallen soldiers. Each stretcher had a flag over the body; I remember the Union Jack, the Rifles flag, and a Liverpool flag. Still to this day, I really struggle to see a Union Jack flag without getting overwhelmed with memories," said McConaghy.

On her final operation, a US medic handed McConaghy a clear plastic bag with the severed foot of an American serviceman killed in action. "It tells me a lot about how my own mental state was by this time of the campaign, as even this didn't make me bat an eyelid or flinch," McConaghy told a reporter.

But McConaghy paid a heavy price for her devotion to duty, and after being discharged from the RAF on medical grounds in 2019, was haunted by post-traumatic stress disorder.

In March, 2020, the United Kingdom entered its first Covid lockdown. McConaghy's coping mechanism of keeping busy with exercise and work came to a grinding halt. She spent days on end in her small apartment binge-eating, getting up in the middle of the night, and searching online for news of any of the soldiers she had deployed with.

"I was hitting self-destruct in spectacular fashion, as many veterans tend to do. Self-sabotage is a well-known symptom that comes with PTSD and depression; we don't just let the wheels come off; we blow the whole damn truck up. No one had any idea how much I was falling apart and how quickly it was gathering pace," McConaghy admitted.

On Wednesday, August 12, 2020, McConaghy woke up and decided that day would be her last day on Earth. She knew she needed assistance and called her doctor in desperation. Sadly, the doctor did not catch onto how dire her situation was and instead prescribed her more anti-depression drugs. Having ordered some other drugs forty-eight hours before, this new batch meant she now had more than enough to end her life.

After calmly writing a suicide note to her family and friends, she began to swallow the one hundred pills, one by one, before closing her eyes for one last time, saying to herself, "My brain is finally at peace."

Her next memory was waking up from a forty-hour coma in a hospital bed. Miraculously, she had survived because after swallowing the pills, she had called emergency services for help.

"It turns out I had actually called at 00:50 in the morning, so clearly something inside me still wanted to fight and live."

This event saved her life as McConaghy started receiving counseling for her PTSD. "I cried for months, finally letting go of all the tears I had stored up inside me over the years that I had never let leak out from my eyes for fear of displaying weakness."

Today, McConaghy states, "PTSD doesn't have to be an anchor around me forever. Just like anything in our body that breaks, with time, rest, and the right people to help us recover, we can mend our broken brains. I've closed the door on that dark tunnel and am walking a new, more positive path."

McConaghy's military career included an impressive seventeen years flying with the RAF's Chinook Fleet. She racked up an incredible three thousand flying hours manning the guns on Chinook helicopters.

"I always describe my time in the Air Force as the best of times and the worst of times, but it's the contrast of both of those that hopefully make for an interesting read in my book."

To read more about Liz McConaghy's incredible life story, please check out her book, "Chinook Crew 'Chick' Highs and Lows of Forces Life from the Longest Serving Female RAF Chinook Force Crewmember."

Source:

How one female Chinook crewman turned her life around after nearly ending it all. https://www.forces.net/mental-health/how-one-female-chinook-crewman-turned-her-life-around-after-nearly-ending-it-all

https://www.helpforheroes.org.uk/our-impact/our-stories/lizs-story/

Read all about Liz's story and how she bounced back from the brink with our help. | Help For Heroes. https://www.helpforheroes.org.uk/our-impact/our-stories/lizs-story/

Women Prisoners of War

Throughout American history, there have been fewer than one hundred military women held as Prisoners Of War. Starting with Florena Budwin, who disguised herself during the Civil War as a man to join Union troops and was held in a Confederate prison camp. During World War II, sixty-seven Army nurses were taken captive by the Japanese. This is just a sample of what they had to endure.

Rhonda Cornum

I looked up, and I saw five Iraqi guys with their, you know, rifles pointed at me. So I knew I wasn't dead... But I knew I was captured.

On February 27, 1991, US Army Flight Surgeon Major Rhonda Cornum remembered it being a cold morning when she awoke on the fourth day of ground fighting during Operation Desert Storm.

Cornum combated the bitterly cold Iraqi morning by zipping up her jacket and drinking a few cups of hot coffee. She was headed out on a routine flight to transport passengers when her Black Hawk Helicopter crew received a call telling them their mission had changed and would now be a rescue. That call changed Cornum's life forever.

Earlier that day, US Air Force fighter pilot Captain Bill Andrews was leading an F-16 flight against heavily defended armor and mechanized forces; Captain Andrews' F-16 suffered significant damage from enemy air defenses, forcing him to eject over enemy territory.

Despite being fired upon by enemy forces during his parachute descent, he made contact with his flight crew using his survival radio. After a hard landing, he broke his leg and suffered several other impact injuries. Exposed in open terrain, Captain Andrews could not move and received incoming fire from encroaching enemy forces.

Cornum's crew was the closest aircraft to Captain Andrews's position, and they were ordered to assist in his rescue. "Unfortunately, we flew right over a big bunker full of weapons, and they shot the tail of our helicopter, and then they shot me," remembered Cornum.

Cornum was only one of three US soldiers to survive the one-hundred-forty-mph helicopter crash. She suffered a bullet wound to her shoulder, two broken arms, and a knee injury.

★★★

After our helicopter crashed, I could not see. It was very dark by this time. It had also been cloudy and smoky when we went in. At that time, I assumed I was the only one that survived... 'cause I didn't see anybody else.

I looked up, and I saw five Iraqi guys with their rifles pointed at me. So I knew I wasn't dead, and I knew I was a prisoner. Then one of them reached down, grabbed me by the arm, and stood me up. And that's when he separated my already broken right arm. And then I knew I was pretty badly hurt.

And so they captured me and, and I got taken down into a bunker and questioned a little about, you know, 'Who are you? What are you doing here?' That type of stuff. And then, they quickly dragged me over to this group of Iraqi soldiers. The group of Iraqi soldiers were standing in a circle, and they opened up and they threw me down in the center next to somebody else. It was Sergeant Dunlap, so I knew there was at least another survivor.

The next part was probably the scariest thing of our entire trip there. Because they just stood there and they put their handguns to the back of our heads, and we really thought they were gonna shoot us. We thought, 'Well, you know, at the end of the war, they're gonna retreat. They don't want prisoners, and this will take care of that problem.' And, you know, who knows what they're thinking.

We both thought we heard them say, 'Shoot em!' And then nothing happened. They dragged us back to our feet and took us down to some other bunker to get interrogated some more.

They realized I was a woman when they stood me up, and at that point, I had my flak jacket on and my survival vest and my weapon, all that stuff, and they started taking all this stuff off. When they took off my helmet, all this long brown hair came out. And until then, I'm sure they just thought I was a skinny guy. But all of a sudden, they realized I was a girl. I don't know what they said, but they were surprised to see me there.

They took us on maybe a thirty-minute truck ride in the dark to Basra. I'm not even sure I knew it was Basra, except that I knew basically where we were going on the mission. I knew that was the only city that was around. And they took us to a prison there. I was just trying to relax, and I don't know; I was just wondering what was happening, and that was when it ... where I got molested.

I was just leaning back on the seat, and all of a sudden, I felt this, this guy sitting next to me put his hands on my face and he started to kiss me. I thought, 'Well, how bizarre! I don't know what he was thinking, but I really thought, Surely he can do better! I mean, I've got a laceration above my eye that's soaked with blood, and I'm sure I don't smell very good. And I'm thinking, how can he possibly want to do this? And then he unzipped my flight suit and started fondling me.

But there really wasn't any way to fight; because of my injuries, I couldn't move anything. I also didn't really want to make him mad; I didn't want to bite him. And so I did nothing. I just sat there. Except when he tried to take me by the back of the head and put my head down in his lap and I couldn't because my arms didn't move then. And the pain was excruciating. I feel confident he knew he shouldn't be doing what he was doing. Because every time I'd scream, he'd quit. So, I think the idea was that the guys in the front of the truck weren't supposed to know.

I suspected that he didn't want to get in trouble. I think if the other guys hadn't been there, he probably wouldn't have stopped either way. But I don't know that. I just was amazed that he would want to do that. My thoughts were also in the hierarchy of bad things happening to me that day; that was pretty low on my list.

Well, next, he stopped and zipped my flight suit back up because we were obviously getting to wherever it was we were going. And I was grateful that it had been a shorter trip than it could've been, I suppose...

★ ★ ★

Cornum was held in a primitive underground jail cell for eight days in what she called austere conditions. On March 6, 1991, Cornum and twenty-three other prisoners of war were released in end-of-war negotiations.

At the request of her chain of command, she initially did not talk about the details of the sexual assault. The Presidential Commission on the Assignment of Women in the Armed Services later asked Cornum to testify about her treatment as a POW. She provided only some details to the commission in that hearing but eventually provided additional details in her book.

To learn more about her story, please check out her book, *She Went to War: The Rhonda Cornum Story.*

Source:

Operation Desert Storm [ushistory.org]. https://www.ushistory.org/US/60a.asp

Female POWs prove women can endure war's hardships | Military Press. https://www.militarypress.com/female-pows-prove-women-can-endure-wars-hardships-2/

Former POW to speak at POW/MIA events - Americus Times-Recorder | Americus Times-Recorder. https://www.americustimesrecorder.com/2015/09/06/former-pow-to-speak-at-powmia-events/

Shoshana Johnson

Shoshana Johnson was raised in a military family, and her father was a twenty-one-year Army vet who served in the first Gulf War. In 1998, Johnson joined the US Army as a Specialist with the 507th Maintenance Company. Her dream after the military was to go to culinary school. In February 2003, Johnson received orders to deploy to Iraq.

On March 23, 2003, during the Battle of Nasiriya, Johnson's convoy was ambushed by Iraqi forces.

★ ★ ★

I remember as we drove, there were some directional mistakes, and they requested us to turn around, and I'm thinking, what the hell's going on? And the guys in my truck were saying, 'We got to get out of here.' They made another mistake, so we had to turn around again, and that's when the ambush started...

It sounded like popcorn or rocks hitting a windshield. Next thing you know, there's a large civilian vehicle that pulls out in front of us. I think it was a dump truck or a tow truck. And we end up going to the side of the road to avoid hitting it. Sergeant

Hernandez, who was driving, tried to get our vehicle out of the area, and we couldn't... We felt a crash; he stuck his head out the window to look around.

One of the convoy's Humvees had crashed into the back of ours, and I could see that we were now pinned in. Sgt. Hernandez and I knew we were in trouble, and we had to get out, so we jumped out of the vehicle. We scrambled underneath the truck to take cover and return fire. I think it's not even a minute underneath that truck when I get shot in both of my legs. Then Sgt. Hernandez gets hit in the arm.

Sgt. Riley joined us and told me his weapon jammed, so I handed him mine. I remember something powerful slamming into the truck, and it's this rocket-propelled grenade. I turned my head and closed my eyes, waiting for it to detonate, but for some reason, it didn't go off.

Next thing you know, Sgt. Hernandez gets pulled out from underneath, and then I feel someone grab my legs and drag me from the vehicle, and they start beating the daylights out of us.

My Kevlar helmet falls off, and they see my braids, and then they step back with an expression on their faces like, WHAT THE HELL, and I guess they realize I'm a female. They rip open up my flak vest, and I'm wearing a t-shirt, so they see boobs, and they're stunned, and then I'm immediately separated. They roughly drag me to one of their vehicles, and violently shove me in, and take off.

The person who pushed me into the vehicle is next to me and he starts checking my pockets and then he gropes me, and I scream, and he slaps me, but he stops groping me.

They brought in a doctor and some other guy. I think he was probably a soldier, and the doctor talked to him, and then they pulled off my boots. Now, that's when the first time I really felt intense pain because he was not careful about it, and the doctor looked over my legs. I asked, 'Am I going to lose my leg?' He speaks like a broken English and says, 'No, soft tissue, soft tissue.' The doctor proceeded to pour iodine on it and wrap it, and then they left me.

It took them quite a while to take us to Baghdad. They stopped in every city to like show us off the captured Americans. By the time we got to Baghdad, it was, I guess, late evening, and the ambush happened in the early morning, so I was exhausted. I was in a lot of pain at that time and they blindfolded and dragged me from room to room. When they took the blindfold off, there was a cameraman all set up with equipment, and there were three other people in there, and they were asking me all these questions.

Then, the Iraqis performed surgery, and they put me under general anesthesia to clean out my wound and do some repairs. I remember they made me sign a release first. I'm like, Yeah, like I have a choice, and they said I could refuse if I want to, and I was like, How am I going to refuse? I'll probably get an infection and die. So, I had the surgery.

As part of the Geneva Convention, you're supposed to separate the males from the females, but as the only female, I'm alone there most of the time and it's hard. The only human contact I had was my guards or the doctor, who would come from time to time to look at my leg.

Sitting there alone gives you a lot of free time to think, and I went through everything I had ever done wrong in my life and apologized to God. I thought a lot about my daughter and God-willing, and if I got a chance to escape or go home, what would I do then. I thought of those friends, those soldiers who I knew were dead, and wondered about the rest of my guys.

In captivity, you don't know what's going to happen from day to day; I wanted to see my daughter grow up and live her life. It's a constant fear because you're in the middle of a combat zone, and you know this country has a history of executing people.

★★★

What Shoshanna didn't know at the time was eleven soldiers from her company had been killed in the ambush in Nasiriyah. Six were also captured. She did eventually learn that she was one of a group of five POWs being held in the Baghdad area.

She also learned later that the Humvee that crashed into the back of their truck had been hit by an RPG. The driver, Lori Ann Piestewa, survived that crash but died later in Iraqi custody. She would be the first female soldier killed in the Iraq War and the first Native American woman in our history to die in combat while serving in the US military.

Supply specialist Jessica Lynch was also in that Humvee. The nineteen-year-old was wounded but survived. Special Operations eventually carried out a nighttime raid on the hospital where Jessica Lynch was being held, and she was rescued. But Shoshana and the others remained in captivity.

Shoshana recalled:

They started moving us from prisons to homes, and that's very scary because the military was checking prisons. You can't go and check every house in a city, so it would be getting harder to find us, and the dread starts setting in.

I remember the night before, they had given us this really cool meal with soda and chocolate, and I thought it was the last meal. They're going to kill us. This is your last, which was stuck in my head, but nope. The Marines came instead to the rescue.

The Marines were approached by an Iraqi, carrying the message that there were some Iraqi soldiers who wanted to surrender, and not only that, the Iraqis wanted to give up the prisoners that they had. Of course, the Marines raced in to grab the seven prisoners and put them on a helicopter and get them back.

Shoshana and the four other Americans had spent twenty-two days as prisoners of war. They were rescued on April 13th, 2003, taken to Kuwait, and then flown to Qatar.

By the time we get to Doha, sure enough, they had it on the news already, and they're trying to get a hold of my family, and they couldn't get through. So they finally got us to the hospital. It was late at night, and they already told me that I was going to have another operation on my legs. Just before they stuck me with morphine, I got a call from my dad.

I didn't think I would break down like that, but as soon as I heard my dad's voice, I broke down and started crying. I remember trying to tell him that I was okay. That I wasn't raped. You know, with Dad, that was going to be a big deal for him, so I tried to say it without saying it.

The next thing was my debriefing. Here, the soldiers have to discuss what they've been through. This is so the military can record what happened, gather intel, and hopefully learn from events. But it's also for the benefit of soldiers who've experienced horror. It's the first time they sit down in a safe, structured environment and begin to process their trauma.

At the time, I didn't see the purpose in it, but it's really best for you to get a lot of things off your chest and just release everything that you've been holding in before you go and meet your family.

They flew us directly to Fort Bliss, so I was going home. And then they told me that there were a lot of people out there, and I was, no problem, it was just my family. Well, there were like two thousand people there, and of course, my family was there too. It was nice that everyone was there to welcome me and give me support, but I just wanted to go home. I didn't really want to deal with it.

I thought I was fine, and I kept saying it. I'm fine. I'm fine. My aunt and my family said, no, you're not, no, you're not. I was different. They expect you to come home the way you left, but that's not possible. You're not the same person. I remember sometimes my dad would be like, 'I want the daughter that I gave to the Army.' I was like, 'She's dead and gone, Dad.'

PTSD with depression is complicated. It's a lot of things. My parents told me that my daughter comes to them talking about how mommy cries all the time and stuff. So, my parents guilted me into being more diligent about my care. I reached a point where I realized that this little girl, my daughter, needs me healthy.

People who work with veterans often tell me this is how they finally convince them to seek help by appealing to that same sense of self-sacrifice that brought them into the military in the first place. This isn't about you or how stoic you think you are. It's about your family. At the local VA health center in El Paso, I get excellent care, but I still have issues. I've been hospitalized three times.

The VA estimates that, in a given year, somewhere between eleven and twenty percent of veterans who served in Iraq or Afghanistan suffer post-traumatic stress. There are effective treatments, but as with many types of physical wounds, managing psychological injury takes time and effort and knowledgeable health care providers. And informally, every veteran I know with PTSD has leaned on other vets for support.

Treating my mental trauma didn't just have an impact on me. It also helped spur other members of my family who were dealing with untreated trauma to finally get help, including my father.

He was different when he came back from war. I don't think he realized that until later on 'cause I pushed him to go through the VA for psychiatric treatment also, and he was diagnosed with PTSD also, but he had never sought treatment; actually, a lot of my relatives that served, it brought up a lot of memories for them.

How do you become normal? That's the question facing every veteran, especially those who have seen combat. You can't unsee the things you saw or undo the things you've done, and even if you could, many wouldn't want to. Most soldiers who've been through combat say the experience showed them they were stronger than they thought they were. It made them feel closer to those they served with and changed their priorities about what is important in life.

I wouldn't change going into the military or being a soldier for anything in the world. The only thing I would change is that day. If I could go back and unring that bell and have all of us come home, that's the one thing I would change. Sometimes you don't realize it until you walk away, and then you are like, damn, I really did have a good time. I remember being in a crisp, ironed uniform, highly shined boots, and extremely puffed out and proud. And I miss that. I really do.

★ ★ ★

Shoshana now volunteers at her church and at the local veteran's clubs. She also finally went to culinary school, courtesy of the GI Bill. Shoshana is a Bronze Star and Purple Heart recipient. She retired with a pension from the Army in 2003, and in 2011, she published *I'm Still Standing: From Captive US Soldier to Free Citizen—My Journey Home.*

Source:

PBS War Story Army.mil/News | By Alexandra Hemmerly-Brown
Published March 09, 2018

Operation Desert Storm [ushistory.org]. https://www.ushistory.org/US/60a.asp

Female POWs prove women can endure war's hardships | Military Press. https://www.militarypress.com/female-pows-prove-women-can-endure-wars-hardships-2/

The Most Inspiring Person of the Year Award -- featuring finalist Archbishop Sean O'Malley - Beliefnet. https://www.beliefnet.com/inspiration/most-inspiring-person-of-the-year/2003/the-most-inpiring-person-of-the-year-award.aspx

American Veteran | Episode 3: The Return | PBS. https://www.pbs.org/video/episode-3-the-return-jekys5/

Lori Piestewa

As the torrent of enemy fire was directed at Lori Piestewa's Humvee, she gunned the engine, accelerating to forty-five mph. She weaved the five-ton military vehicle as best as she could to avoid the worst of the incoming bullets.

She had just turned to go around a disabled trailer when a rocket-propelled grenade streaked through the air, hitting the vehicle's front left tire. With no way to control the Humvee, it crashed into the back of the disabled trailer.

Lori Piestewa was the first female United States Soldier to be killed in the Iraq War. She is also believed to be the first Native American woman to be killed while participating in modern-day combat. Her hometown of Tuba City, Arizona, dedicated a local mountain peak to be renamed in her honor.

The Piestewa family had a long tradition of military service; her paternal grandfather served in the US Army in World War II, and her father was drafted into the Army in 1965 and served in combat during the Vietnam War.

Born on December 14, 1979, Lori's Hopi Tribe name was Kocha-Hon-Mana, or White Bear Girl. Life was tough growing up on the reservation, with high unemployment and few job options. Being strong-willed and independent, Lori hated the idea of being a young adult single mom living with her parents and having them help her and her children with bills.

Besides Piestewa's family history of serving their country, Lori saw the military as a way to support her children and help her achieve her dream of going to college. Lori signed up for the Army in late 2001. When her unit deployed to Iraq, Lori was medically held back. She had severely injured her shoulder in a training exercise and was just recovering from surgery.

With her strong sense of duty, Lori went to her supervisors and argued to allow her to deploy with her comrades. They agreed only if she could convince her doctor to sign off early that her injury was fully healed. Lori toughed it out through her medical clearance exam and was given permission to deploy with her unit.

Lori served as a member of the US Army's 507th Maintenance Company, a support unit comprised of repair and maintenance personnel. On March 23, 2003, Lori was driving a Humvee on a convoy mission. The main convoy, with the smaller and faster vehicles, had left two hours earlier before the rest of the heavy military trucks.

The Supply Company was now at half strength, deep in hostile territory, and without the protection of the forward battalion. During the mission, Pfc. Jessica Lynch's truck broke down, and she got into the Humvee that Lori was driving. The convoy was traveling through the desert and was meant to bypass the town of Nasiriyah, but it got lost and was caught in an ambush.

After being hit by a rocket-propelled grenade and crashing, Lori, Shoshana Johnson, and Jessica Lynch all survived the crash with serious injuries. Three other soldiers in the Humvee died that day. They were taken prisoner along with four others.

Al Jazeera television later aired a video showing Lori and several of the other prisoners of War inside an Iraqi hospital.

In an excerpt from Jessica Lynch's book, *I'm a Soldier, Too: The Jessica Lynch Story,* she claimed that Lori sustained a severe head wound during the incident. The Iraqi doctors were possibly unable to perform surgery due to equipment limitations, including intermittent power grid electrical issues.

The Piestewa family watched television news interviews of people in her unit being interviewed by Iraqi TV, and for more than a week, they waited, hoping for any news. All around her hometown, signs were hung out reading, "Put your porch light on, show Lori the way home."

On April 1, 2003, US Marines and Navy SEALs, under the command of the Army, staged a diversionary attack to draw any Iraqi soldiers away from the Hospital in Nasiriyah. Meanwhile, an element from the Joint Special Operations Task Force 121 launched a nighttime raid on the hospital and successfully retrieved Lynch but were unable to locate Lori.

The Army declared her as Missing In Action. Lynch's subsequent recovery was the first successful rescue of an American prisoner of War since World War II and the first ever of a woman.

Special Forces later discovered a mass shallow grave near the hospital. One of the bodies that was later positively identified was Lori Piestewa. She had apparently survived the crash but died at the hospital a short time later. It is unclear when, how, or why she died.

Lori Piestewa was only twenty-three years old at the time of her death. After her death, Piestewa was posthumously promoted to Specialist, and later that year, the Grand Canyon State Games became the Lori Piestewa Games in honor of her love of sports.

Source:

Warriors In Uniform. http://warriorsinuniform.com/teachers/

Hunter, Frogman, Sniper, Spy: Retired SEAL Terry Houin Is Just Getting Started. https://coffeeordie.com/sniper-terry-houin

American History « Alphabet Local – Your Mobile Ads Leader!. https://alplocal.com/american-history/

Jessica Lynch: Her War, Her Story - Military Women's Memorial. https://womensmemorial.org/jessica-lynch/

Frances Liberty

If they're going to die, let them see an American woman that looks and smells good."

—Frances M. Liberty

For my final story, I wanted to dedicate it to someone truly extraordinary—someone who rises above even this remarkable collection of war heroes. A figure who embodies the very essence of courage, resilience, and selflessness—the qualities that define a hero, no matter their gender.

That's why I chose to honor the fearless, humble, and tough-as-nails US Army Lieutenant Colonel Frances M. Liberty. A woman who never minced words and never backed down, her incredible career spanned World War II, the Korean War, the Cold War, and three grueling tours in Vietnam. She wasn't just a witness to history—she shaped it with unwavering dedication and an unbreakable spirit.

Her journey through the tumultuous and often dangerous environments of these global conflicts was marked by a deep commitment to serving her country and the patients under her care. She survived World War II as a participant in the first landings in Anzio, Italy. She endured enemy attacks in Korea, sapper attacks in Vietnam, a helicopter crash in the jungle, venomous snakes, giant lizards, and more diseases with unpronounceable names than I can list on one page.

Her humility, which was matched only by her sense of duty, was revealed when she refused to accept the Purple Heart, a medal for being wounded. Despite being hit by shrapnel and sustaining minor injuries in an attack in Vietnam, she told her superiors, "Purple Hearts should only go to the soldiers who fight in combat with more serious injuries!"

★★★

My name is Frances Liberty, and I was born on January 9, 1923, in Plattsburgh, New York. If you've never heard of Plattsburgh, we sit close to Lake Champlain and are about a five-hour drive from New York City.

Plattsburgh's roots go back to 1784 when Zephaniah Platt obtained 33,000 acres of land. In 1785, the Platts and a group of settlers started building their cabins and mills. In 1902, this small town officially became a city.

Our most famous battle occurred in 1814 in what's known as the Battle of Plattsburgh Bay. Our cemetery holds the graves of American and British soldiers killed in the fighting, and we honor both sides. As George Washington once said, "Every post is honorable in which a man can serve his country."

My story begins with my journey into the military. I can still clearly remember the day I stood with my heavy duffel bag strapped over my shoulder, looking over at the women like me who had also chosen to enlist in the US Army Nurse Corps. I wondered if they were as nervous as I was. The reality of the path we had chosen was a dangerous one.

As a child, I loved taking care of others. I had always pictured myself in a prim and proper uniform, walking with purpose toward someone in need. But life had other plans. While I was still in nurse training, World War II broke out.

Under normal circumstances, the war would have had little to do with me. But nothing was normal in those times. People were dying on the field, and many of these deaths could have been prevented if they had received timely medical treatment. The desperate need for nurses led to an unusual decision by the governing body; the board agreed to allow nurses in training to take the state board exams early.

At 20, I took the state board exam, and when I returned home that day, I told my father I was thinking of joining the Army. I didn't know what his reaction would be, but the look on his face told me all I needed to hear. He was not happy—he hated it.

"No, you are not," he said firmly, his deep baritone voice echoing the finality.

I listened to all his objections but knew he'd eventually come to terms with it. That day, as a young know-it-all, I walked away from our conversation with even more determination to join the Army. I'll show him, I stubbornly thought, and I immediately went downtown and enlisted in the Army Nurse Corps.

When I broke the news the next day to my father, there was no anger at all. His eyes dropped, and his face became solemn as he exhaled a long, deep breath. With a heavy heart, he simply said calmly, expressionlessly, "You've made your bed; now lie in it."

My introduction to this new world began at Fort Dix, where the others and I went through the basic training program. Many of us were fresh out of nursing school, utterly unprepared for the realities of war. If we were to save lives on the battlefield, we first had to learn how to survive. The dead can't save the dying.

Fort Dix was barely designed for women. The Army itself seemed unsure of how to handle female recruits.

Basic training meant scaling walls, hiking, crawling through mud, and maneuvering under barbed wire while officers fired their guns above us. The loud sound of their guns made us scamper to safety. I quickly learned to keep my head down.

Once, a sergeant handed me a bag of rocks and ordered me to carry it in my left hand—to "teach me to step out on my left foot." I left the training ground with stiff joints and a sore body that day; I could barely feel my hands when I finally dropped the bag of rocks.

There was little time for rest. The training seemed a little too rigorous to be called basic, pushing many of us to reconsider our decision to enlist in the Army.

Fort Dix was clearly different from the structured and conservative environment of the Catholic hospital I was used to. It took me a while to adjust to the idea of taking showers with strangers; such acts were unheard of where I came from.

Enduring the exhausting physical demands of my new life in the Army was a lot for me to deal with, but as if the training wasn't tough enough, we had to work in the wards, learning the routines of military nurses.

After a brief stop at Camp Patrick Henry in Virginia, I found myself on a ship bound for Europe. I knew my life would change when I enlisted, but I hadn't fully grasped how much. With only a few months in, I was already traveling to the other end of the world.

There I was, a young girl with an oversized helmet struggling to sit on my head, hauling sixty pounds of medical supplies on my back, tightening my grip on the duffel bag in my left hand, walking up a gangplank to board a freighter named *Liberty*. I took it as a sign. Maybe this was my destiny. Maybe God was showing me I was on the right path. Or maybe not.

At the head of the gangplank, I called out my last name, middle name, and serial number, as those before me had done.

"Liberty Frances, MN 799507," I hollered, adjusting my grip on my duffel bag.

The officer glanced at his list, then back at me, his forehead creasing. He gasped, "Oh my God, you're a woman!"

"Last time I checked," I answered.

I had no idea why he was so shocked. I had never seen anyone startled at the fact that I was a woman.

"You got billed with the men," he muttered.

Someone had misspelled *Frances* as *Francis*. I stared at him, unsure of what to do with that information. I just stood there looking at him, holding up the line.

"Go stand over there," he finally ordered.

My back ached as I tightened my grip on my duffel bag and hurried out of the line. As I stood there watching the other soldiers board the freighter, I saw a tall, elegant woman approach me. She was in uniform, so I could tell she was in the Army. It was hard to imagine someone with so much poise opting to join the Army—it didn't seem logical.

Later, I found out that this tall, statuesque woman was the chief nurse, a former nurse director before joining the Army. Maybe some of us preferred to take the long and tedious road to success.

"Don't move," she said as she walked past me.

I had no idea where I could possibly go, certainly not back down the gangplank. The heart palpitations I had when I was boarding the freighter were enough to give me a heart attack.

As I contemplated my fate, another nurse joined me in the corner.

"They got you mixed with the men too?" I asked quietly.

"Yes," she sighed.

"They misspelled your name?"

"My name is Marian," she grumbled. "Apparently, that's a man's name in the South."

"At least they got your name right," I tried to smile.

Neither of us liked our situation, but I was determined to make the best of it. If I was going to lie in the bed I made, like my father said, I had better find a way to get comfortable. They had to find a way to accommodate us; there was obviously no way we were going to be sleeping in the men's room.

Interestingly, someone came up with the creative idea of rigging hammocks between the bunks in the cramped stateroom. There were four bunks in each room, and unfortunately for me, all four of my roommates were seasick. I could not afford to join them; I had to avoid the room like the plague.

I spent my first night in the hallway; the fear of catching whatever they had kept me sitting up all night.

By the second night, I became curious about the people I saw climbing up and down the stairs in the hallway. This curiosity led me to take those stairs. I had no idea what I would find, but I silently hoped it wouldn't lead me to a room filled with seasick people. As I snuck up the stairs, I noticed another girl following me closely. Her room was down the hall, and I had seen her in the hall the night before.

We quietly crawled behind a gun placement, curling against each other to keep warm. The cold was brutal. We were on the Atlantic in October; the wind had no mercy. I preferred the cold deck to a room full of seasick people. However, our momentary comfort was short-lived. I could hear footsteps advancing toward us.

Two seamen found us. After an awkward silence and a staring contest, one finally said, "You can stay, but don't make a sound."

"And for God's sake, don't light a match and give away our position to the enemy," his companion added.

A sigh of relief escaped from my mouth when I heard them walk away. We were lucky. The idea of the seamen sending us back to our rooms scared the living daylight out of me.

The next night, we stealthily climbed up the stairs again. When we got to our spot, we found two pillows and blankets waiting for us. It was the kindest gesture I had experienced since joining the Army. Thanks to our hidden spot, neither of us got seasick.

When we finally got to England, it was comforting to stand on solid ground. But that relief was short-lived. Barely a few hours after we arrived, I was reassigned to a unit bound for Africa. I was taken out of the group from New York because I had more experience. As the only Yankee in the group, I was skeptical about the kind of reception I would get. At this point, it had finally dawned on me that I was far from home.

After a month in Africa, we were suddenly ordered onto these little boats—the LSTs—in the middle of the night. I remember it was right around the third week of January 1944. The LSTs were landing ship tanks used by the Navy to transport troops and vehicles onto the beaches. Most people have seen them in pictures of the D-Day landings.

We boarded the boats without asking any questions; the mumblings and murmurings in the crowd made some of us anxious. Before we knew it, our boats docked in Anzio, Italy. We landed close to 50,000 men and a handful of us women.

The procedure was to march out of the boats and wait for orders from our superiors. The sight of us startled the commanding officer, a huge colonel whose physical features were possibly that of a giant. "My God! You're women!" he bellowed at our chief nurse, his fear poorly masked by his stern demeanor. "You're not supposed to be here yet."

The colonel looked like he was going to blow his top. Apparently, we arrived too soon. We were supposed to be part of the third wave, but we somehow found ourselves in the first wave. We didn't know if this was a good or a bad sign, but the colonel certainly didn't look pleased. Our chief nurse squared her shoulders, placed her hands on her hips, met his gaze, and declared, "We're here now, so deal with it." The colonel was actually amused. He could not believe that a half-sized woman would talk back to him. But our chief nurse didn't back down, so the colonel had to comply.

There was little resistance from the Germans during our landing, so we established a beachhead with our allies seven miles deep. When our troops tried to advance from the beachhead, the Germans responded in full force, and the fight was on.

A week after we landed, the Germans called in reinforcements and had about 71,000 soldiers to our 61,000 Allied troops. The terrain on that Anzio beach was rough to move around because it was mostly low-lying marshland with little to no vegetation.

The badly drained soil caused our trenches to quickly fill with water. There was little cover for our troops besides our foxholes. The Luftwaffe fighter planes also hit us hard on bombing runs. The Royal Navy, which had been giving us some cover earlier in the week with their big guns, had to withdraw due to the accuracy of the German fighter pilots with their missile attacks.

The German artillery was also deadly. They had this gigantic 280mm railway gun nicknamed Anzio Annie that pounded away at us on the beachhead.

For the next five months, we lived and worked in these muddy foxholes. In that first week, I realized why the Army told me to keep my fanny down—shrapnel and bullets were constantly whizzing by. We had to crawl to the other foxholes to drag the injured. The Army eventually had to build larger foxholes because the initial ones could no longer accommodate all the injured military and civilian personnel.

We were young. We were passionate about our job on the field but, at the same time, a bit reckless, and that zeal contributed to the loss of seven of our nurses. Casualties were unavoidable, but we silently hoped that everyone would make it out alive. It was a costly battle, with close to 24,000 US troops and 10,000 British troops killed. Most people only know about the Normandy invasion—Operation Overlord—but Anzio was a rough place, too. On June 5, 1944, the battle was effectively over, with the Allies capturing Rome.

One of the hardest things I had to do at Anzio was drag back the lifeless bodies of our nurses into those foxholes. These were young women in their twenties who had a promising future. By the end of World War II, a total of sixteen Army Nurse Corps volunteers would be killed as a result of direct enemy fire. Sixty-eight American servicewomen were captured as POWs in the Philippines.

Hitler gave many speeches back then, calling Americans degenerates for putting their women to work. The role of German women, he would often proclaim, was to be wives and mothers and have more babies for the Third Reich.

Well, luckily, Hitler's stupidity was the Allies' strength. Our women served in the military, worked in defense plants, and volunteered for war-related organizations. When our men left to fight, our women became stronger and more productive. We managed finances at home; we learned to fix the car and appliances. That commitment—utilizing all of the United States assets, including women—is what made us so powerful.

Luckily, some of us made it out of Anzio unscathed. We were heading for Rome, but we made several stops at camps to refill their medical supplies. Whenever we stopped, I had a chance to interact with our soldiers. Many of them were still very enthusiastic, while others had that thousand-yard stare.

Our trip to Rome wasn't without a notable incident, but it displayed our chief nurse's beautiful camaraderie and character. On the trip, there were no bathrooms; all they had were these slit trenches. As women in slacks, we couldn't use the slit trench. Our chief nurse had built some kind of reputation among the officers as a bit of a hell-raiser.

We were not surprised when she walked up to the commanding officer and flatly told him, "The girls can't use that; it's a slit trench. Do you have any other options?"

"Well, tell 'em to deal with it," the commanding officer waved in a bid to dismiss her. It took a minute, but I knew there was going to be a stinging comeback.

"My ladies are sitters, not pointers. Fix it," she said with a stern voice before walking away. Did he fix it? Of course, he did. And we were not surprised.

We finally got to Rome, and we used one of Mussolini's summer palaces as our makeshift hospital. The trip to Rome had a few bumps in the road, but the stay was wonderful. At the hospital, we used one of Mussolini's bathtubs as a Hubbard tank for orthopedic injuries, and the palace was very close to St. Peter's, which made it easier for me to attend mass every day.

While we were in Rome, the war was finally coming to an end. We were there when the Pope came out for the first time since the war started. I could not believe my eyes. I remember going to see the Pope with a friend. We were kneeling in the mud with tears running down our faces uncontrollably. It was a sight to behold. I would argue that it was a perfect ending to one of the worst years in history.

I finally got the chance to go home. At the end of the war, I got out of the Army—or I thought I got out of the Army. I saved lives and helped a lot of people, but I didn't want to remain in the Army. I wanted to be back home with my family. When I left, I thought I was discharged. I had a good run, but I didn't want to go back there. The plan was to start my life on a fresh sheet.

Back home, I had no trouble getting a job as a night supervisor at Leonard Hospital. I was happy and content with my new life. But my happiness was cut short when I got a letter stating I would be called back into the Army.

I found out that the Army, in its infinite wisdom, had a strategy to keep a reserve. When you get out of the Army on a Monday, Wednesday, or Friday, you are separated. You are only discharged when you get out on a Tuesday, Thursday, or Saturday. Imagine my luck. I thought I was discharged when I wasn't. I was separated.

It was hard to come to terms with the fact that I was going back to the world of chaos. But the Korean conflict was heating up, and I got called back into the game. Before I was shipped to Korea, my father was in the hospital; his heart was bad. I was hoping the Army would let me stay back to take care of him. It was the only way I could get out of being called back into the Army. But the Army didn't budge; they told me he had other daughters in the area who could take care of him.

I went to see my father before I left for Korea.

"Pop, I'm going to have to go."

He said with a tenderness I had never heard before, "You have the talent that our country needs right now. I'm very proud of you." He squeezed my hands gently. It was a full-circle moment for me. I left my father's bedside that day with a heavy heart.

★★★

214

After five years of building tensions on the Korean Peninsula, the Korean War officially started on June 25, 1950. The North Korean People's Army crossed the 38th parallel and invaded South Korea. The North Koreans' goal was to unify all of Korea under the North Korean communist government.

President Harry Truman believed the Soviet Union and Communist China encouraged and helped supply this invasion. In an effort to stop the spread of communism, Truman committed U.S. military forces to the coalition of United Nations forces assisting the Republic of Korea in its defense.

Throughout the Korean War, Frances rode the hospital trains, transporting wounded soldiers from mobile army surgical hospitals (MASH units) to various station hospitals. The harsh terrain, the constant threat of enemy fire, and the overwhelming number of casualties placed tremendous strain on the military's medical resources. Yet, Liberty's resourcefulness shone through as she expertly navigated the difficulties of triage, ensuring that limited medical supplies were utilized efficiently and that the most urgent cases received care first. Her ability to remain calm under pressure, even when faced with the most dire situations, further cemented her reputation as a capable and compassionate leader.

Frances, known in the Korean War as "Colonel Libby," remarked on her time in Korea by stating, "Don't believe the TV stuff about MASH units—that's not real!"

Although Frances didn't talk much in interviews about her time in Korea, she did go into great detail about her time in Vietnam and described it as the following:

During my time in the Army, I moved around a lot, but the most remarkable experience was my time in Vietnam. I had been there for a while, but this time, I was sent to Cam Ranh Bay. It was a large hospital that housed patients who were in recovery; the hospital also served as the main blood bank for all of Vietnam.

Surprisingly, the hospital was built of concrete brick, which was almost unheard of in Vietnam. You could barely find anything made of brick there at that time. The entire building was underground. The hospital was a big deal in Vietnam.

While I was stationed at Cam Ranh Bay, they had to keep us hidden, which also explains why the hospital was underground. For a hospital like that, it's a no-brainer that we'd be targeted. I was sleeping in the trailer because I had to leave the bunkers for the young soldiers; they needed them more than I did.

One morning, I woke up with my back against the trailer, and a bright light shone in front of me. The trailer had a big window, and I could see the light from it. At that moment, I thought it was the sun and that I had overslept.

We always had to sleep in our clothes, with our boots turned upside down so bugs wouldn't crawl into them. When what I thought was the reflection of the sun hit my face, I put my boots on hurriedly and stepped outside.

Suddenly, I heard the sentry guard shout, "Colonel, get down!"

"What's going on?" I asked, scanning the area quickly.

"Colonel, get down!" he screamed again. But I couldn't figure out what the problem was.

When I didn't move fast enough, he tackled me, and I went down with my face in the sand.

"You better have a damn good reason for that," I said, furious.

"We're under attack. That bright light you see? That's our barracks being blown up," he said, gasping for air.

This happened right after President Johnson made a speech declaring Cam Ranh Bay the safest place in the world. We had no arms or sentries posted—except for a few stationed at the nurses' quarters.

I said to the guard, "I need to get down to the emergency room."

And to get to the emergency room, we had to crawl through a ditch. I hated every second of it because I hated bugs, and I had to deal with the big cockroaches and other insects as I tried to maneuver my way there. The sentry tried to cover me with his body as we crawled.

"Colonel, if anything happens to you, they're going to kill me," he said quietly.

I told him, "If anything happens to me, you'll probably be dead too."

But we were lucky that day. The Air Force stationed at Cam Ranh Bay came to rescue us, and Navy ships coming in from night patrol saw the fire and pulled in to help.

Before they got to us, the Navy called in to ask if they could assist, but they were told they needed permission from the village chief. They floated in anyway. The Air Force nurses and some of the doctors helped rescue some of the patients, but unfortunately, we lost many wounded men in that attack. It made me so angry; these were men who were already hospitalized.

In Vietnam, we often pulled soldiers straight from the field; sometimes, they were still carrying ammunition. We got them from the Delta, covered in mud and slime, and had to use a water hose to wash them off. One day, a high-ranking officer from Washington was visiting while I was working triage. I didn't enjoy sitting behind a desk in the office; I preferred working out there with the others.

"Do you really have to use a hose?" the high-ranking officer from Washington asked.

"What do you suggest?" I was curious.

"Oh, there must be something else," she answered.

I told her, "Go back to Washington, sit behind your nice little desk, and think of something. When you do, notify us, and we'll be sure to do it."

"Are you trying to be sarcastic?" she asked.

"Yes, I am. Darling, don't get too close; you might get dirty," I answered.

The hardest thing for Americans to learn in Vietnam was triage—not understanding it, but practicing it. In our culture, we take care of the worst injuries first, but in Vietnam, we had to learn how to treat the walking wounded first.

We focused on the ones who only needed one doctor for surgery; that way, we could get 20 or 30 treated quickly. The badly injured were stabilized with fluids and pain medications until the doctors were free. Sometimes, it took two or three doctors to attend to one critical patient.

One day, I was flying in a helicopter with six young nurses and the chief nurse of the Army. Suddenly, we got hit mid-air. The rear gunner and the co-pilot were both injured, but miraculously, we didn't crash. We managed to land in the jungle, and as we sat there, all I could think was, Dear God. The young nurses were screaming, terrified, obviously shaken. I did my best to calm them down.

Once they were somewhat under control, I turned to the chief nurse, whom I knew personally.

"Are you alright?" I asked.

"Yes," she nodded; her face looked pale but steady.

"You know we'll need to get out of here," I told her. "And we'll probably have to walk."

The co-pilot had an arm injury; I had to give him first aid and put his arm in a sling. The rear gunner was in worse shape and had to be carried out. Luckily, we had litters. We got the litters out and put him in it. The six nurses stood around, looking at me, then at each other. I could tell they were hesitant. Finally, one of them spoke up.

"I didn't join the Army to carry litters. I'm a nurse."

I looked her straight in the eye and said, "Well, you're either going to take turns carrying it, or you're going to share it with him."

That settled it. The nurses got on with it, taking turns as we made our way through the jungle. As we walked, I spotted something moving among the trees. A massive lizard—so big, it looked like a dragon to me. I nudged the pilot walking beside me.

"Look at that thing."

He glanced over and shrugged. "Don't worry, they're herbivores."

Pointing at the lizard, I asked, "Yeah? But does he know that?"

The co-pilot was a few steps ahead of us. Then the pilot turned to me and asked, "You want a gun, Lib?"

I raised an eyebrow and asked him, "What will I do with that? I'm afraid of them."

As we walked on, we heard some noise ahead of us, and instinctively, we got into a ditch. My heart was pounding. Oh my God, I thought. I can't let these young nurses be taken prisoner. Then, through the trees, we could see figures emerging. We saw that it wasn't the enemy but a US Marine patrol. They had seen our chopper go down and had come looking for us. I had never been so relieved to see anyone in my life.

Well, those Marines were probably happier than we were. Can you imagine these guys fighting in the jungles day and night only to come upon a group of young American nurses?

After finishing her last tour in Vietnam, Frances Liberty officially retired from the military in 1971. She served a total of 27 years in service to our country and settled in East Greenbush, NY.

I'd like to end Frances Liberty's incredible biography with her favorite story, one she often retold about a wounded soldier whose chances of survival were very slim.

While serving in Vietnam, I was in the triage area with a severely injured soldier, reading his chart. I absently began reciting the rosary.

The soldier opened his eyes, looked up at me, and asked, "What's that noise?"

You know, when you're dying, or when you're that close to death, your hearing is more acute.

I said to him, "I'm saying my rosary beads."

He said, "You don't read, do you?"

I said, "Yes, I do, and very well, thank you."

He said, "Well, I'm Jewish."

I asked him, "But do you believe in God?"

He said, "Yes."

And I said, "Well, it's the same guy."

So we sat there for a while. He was really abrupt, but he was dying, so he had a good reason to be a little irritable. Pretty soon, the orderly came in and started to take him into surgery.

As I was getting up to leave, he said to me, "Hey, you know what? Let me have those beads. They may be lucky."

I said, "Oh, they're more than lucky."

So I gave him the beads and chalked them up to another pair of rosary beads lost because I lost a lot of them that way. The next day, I was in the hall when one of the nurses came over to me and said, "You know that last guy we took, the one that didn't look like he was going to make it?"

I said, "Yes."

She told me he did better than the others, and he was already being shipped to Japan.

Several months later, I was working in another hospital when I got a package. I don't know how this guy found me, but inside was a new pair of rosary beads. A note in the package said that he was keeping the original.

Fast forward another twenty or thirty years, and I'm home and retired now. I get a phone call. I don't know how this guy keeps finding me, but he does. He's in New York, and he's the vice president of a big bank.

He said, "I just want you to know that your rosary beads are kept safe in an ashtray on my desk. And nobody in my office has a clue why I keep them there."

And then he added one last thing, "I just had a granddaughter born in Israel, and she's named Liberty Ann."

I said, "How could you do that to a kid?"

He said, "I always talked about you to my kids, how you saved my life, and my son wanted his daughter to have your name."

After hanging up the phone, I sat stunned. And then I cried.

On March 1, 2004, at 80 years old, Lt. Col. Frances Mary Liberty passed away in Troy, Rensselaer County, New York. She is buried in Saint Mary's Cemetery in the same town.

A hero's life often, and sadly, comes with a silent price. In Lt. Col. Liberty's case, she may never have known how many soldiers she saved and comforted—how many wounded soldiers whose hands she held, how many smiles she mustered through pain and agony. There were just... too many to remember.

A hero never sees their actions as heroic or incredible. They just see a job that needs to be done, so they do it, regardless of the dangers. To those lives that a hero never sees again, they can only hope for the best—that they lived a good life, raised a family, and passed away in peace.

God bless Frances M. Liberty.

Source:

History At a Glance: Women in World War II | The National WWII Museum | New Orleans. https://www.nationalww2museum.org/students

(2015). 164th Infantry News: July 2015.

Library of Congress

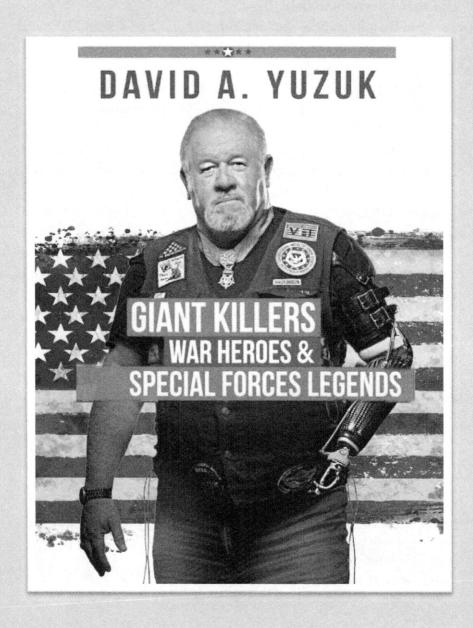

...his helicopter violently crashed, he was blown up, shot and stabbed by a bayonet but somehow kept fighting! —US Army Specialist Fourth Class Medal of Honor Recipient Gary G. Wetzel

Gary Wetzel risked his life and sacrificed his limb in the name of saving as many men as he could. Despite suffering extensive wounds that might've killed another, when duty called, he answered.

Soldiers in Vietnam were not in a rush to become door gunners. Compared to most other occupations, hanging part way out the door of a helicopter as a living target seemed like a bad career path to most. What's the lifespan of a door gunner? Five minutes — or so said the popular legend at the time. While the real-life span of a door gunner in Vietnam was longer than five minutes, within every legend is a kernel of truth, and being a door gunner meant your machine gun was the only thing between you and the enemy. But those odds never stopped Gary Wetzel.

It was January 8, 1968, and then-Pfc. Gary G. Wetzel was on duty and onboard a helicopter near Ap Dong An in the Republic of Vietnam. According to his interview from the Library of Congress Veterans History Project, they were on an "eagle flight," named because they'd fly over an area waiting to catch something happening on the ground or looking off and then react to it.

They had already made a few stops: dropping off their deadly cargo of seven or eight troops, scanning the area, scooping them up again, and leaving. Nothing had happened until the first bad omen reared its head. While grounded at an old French fort to meet with a ground commander, a group of Australian helicopters joined them, a number of them shot nearly to pieces. After that, decisions were made by the higher-ups, and Wetzel was back on the helicopter as part of an insertion force of both American and Australian choppers.

A short time later, Wetzel's helicopter was flying over the area of the air strike, getting ready to open up its doors and let the machine gun rip. In his interview with the Library of Congress, Wetzel described the job of the door gunner as laying down enough covering fire that enemies can't fire back at you or your brothers-in-arms. "You try to keep Charlie's head down to eliminate, you know, casualties as much as you can. And anyone with any common sense, you hear — you hear a bang-bang-bang — you're not going to stick your head up and look; you're going to duck." Wetzel was ready to do his job, but nobody was prepared for what happened next.

The standard procedure for a mission like this was to have more than one set of gunships closely staggered so they could cover each other. You can imagine how thick the tension felt in the hot Vietnamese air when Wetzel's helicopter started dropping into the treetops, committing to the fight — and their backup was a quarter mile behind them.

Wetzel states that this was when he realized the situation was a "big god-damn mistake." Now 15–20 feet off the ground, a barrage of gunfire immediately erupted as numerous Viet Cong stood up from their hiding places, Wetzel describing it as feeling like there "must have been eight million of 'em stood up." In an instant, they were caught in a hailstorm of gunfire — and then came the rocket-propelled grenade. From ahead and left of the helicopter, the RPG made a direct hit, blowing out the front of the ship.

What Wetzel did afterward was extraordinary, but the scenario he and the rest of the crew found themselves in was, unfortunately, very common. According to the Vietnam Helicopter Pilots Association, of the more than 12,000 helicopters operating in Vietnam, over 5,000 were destroyed by combat or accidents.

But dig into the stats and the stories, and you'll find out why Vietnam was "the helicopter War," as retired Maj. Gen. Carl H. McNair described it. In addition to their incredible offensive capabilities, helicopters were used in more than 850,000 medical evacuation missions conducted during that War, and they did incredible work boosting the survival rates of wounded soldiers.

Right now, though, it was Wetzel and his crew that needed rescuing. After scraping to a halt on the ground and being lit up by withering crossfire — all in the span of a few seconds — two of the men were already dead. Snapping into action, Wetzel was determined to save as many as he could and decided to start by ensuring his aircraft commander was safe.

When he threw open the door separating them, his commander was in terrible shape — but alive. He and his crew chief managed to get the commander out of the devastated helicopter. Then disaster struck. "And we got him about halfway up, and then Bart says duck, and then he goes like this — and I hear a bang." Before he knew what had happened, he was blown into a rice paddy by two enemy explosives that went off just inches from his location.

His left arm — gone. He had severe wounds on his right arm, chest, and left leg. Profuse bleeding. War is hell, and Wetzel was in the ninth circle of it. Despite all of this, he had no chance for hesitation; looking over his left side, he spotted a VC gripping another grenade, his body betraying his intention to toss it right at Wetzel. One-armed yet single-minded, Wetzel whipped his Thompson around and zippered him up. The stunned VC fell back, his explosive going off and killing multiple hostiles clustered around him. More explosives went off. It was a spectacular, chaotic light show of lethality.

"It's like the fourth of July, but it's on the ground. And you don't get to see the colors, you don't get to say ooh and ah; you just shit in your pants."

Wetzel and another man raced to their aircraft commander and put tourniquets on his legs, staunching the flow of blood.

At that moment, Bart, the other conscious man, warned Wetzel that the Vietnamese were flooding the area and killing the wounded. Knowing his limits, knowing he couldn't take them all with brute force, Wetzel and the two other men opted to feign death. They certainly looked the part: Wetzel was missing an arm and sprawled out in muddy water, Bart with holes in his head and missing part of his jaw from shrapnel, the aircraft commander being so close to the light at the end of the tunnel he just rolled over.

Wetzel heard footfalls ... a boot stomped down in front of him, his one eye peeking out of the muddy water being the only sense he had of his surroundings. He's just waiting for the shot to come, making his peace, thinking the VC should just get it over with. The shot comes, but it goes through his foot. We can only speculate why the enemy would shoot Wetzel anywhere but the head, but what we do know is that he wouldn't live to see the error of his ways. Shots rang out, these now from Americans, and the VC hurried away.

Wetzel figured he'd had enough rest and was ready for more action; he snatched his Thompson and crawled around the chopper. He saw the VC trying to unfix the machine gun from the helicopter — his machine gun — and, raising up his Thompson, blew the six enemies off their feet and into their graves. Wetzel returned to his aircraft commander, who said one of the hardest things a man can hear: to tell his wife he loves her.

"I'm like, 'shut up, you tell her yourself, we'll get out of this shit, you know.'"

The anger started welling up inside Wetzel, but he didn't have time to cry; he reacted with action — with a vengeance. He tucked his useless, mangled arm into his waistband to keep it from flopping around and did what he described as his "John Wayne run," putting bursts of .45 rounds into anyone in his way as he dashed for the helicopter. He took some lead in the leg and went down on one knee ... and the next thing he remembers was having miraculously staggered back to his original position in the helicopter's gunwell.

Fueled by sheer willpower and making use of what little blood he had left running through his veins, he overcame the shock and wracking pain of his injuries and full-pulled the trigger. At that moment, his machine gun was the only weapon that was being used effectively against the enemy. Wetzel remained in place, pouring bullets onto the enemy weapons emplacement until they stopped firing back.

There was no time to stop. Refusing to tend to his own grievous wounds, he attempted to return to the aid of his aircraft commander. Unfortunately, the body has its limits, and Wetzel's was long past the breaking point. Massive blood loss left him passed out on the ground. But not for long. Regaining consciousness, he snapped back into doing what he believed to be his duty, dragging himself to the aid of his fellow crewman.

After agonizing effort, he came to the side of the crew chief, who was attempting to drag the wounded aircraft commander to a nearby dike, the safest place they could find. Amid all this, Wetzel passed out again, and again, he pulled himself up to his feet, unwavering in his devotion to his brothers. He continued on, grabbing other wounded soldiers and pulling them across the rice paddy. It would be more than 10 hours before reinforcements would begin to evacuate the wounded.

Wetzel survived, but his left arm had to be amputated. After six months in the hospital, he transitioned back into civilian life. While working as an expeditor in Wisconsin sometime later, he had some unusual guests show up to his workplace.

A colonel, a major, and a first sergeant all had a message to deliver: he'd be going on a trip soon. At the time, Wetzel brushed it off — he'd already gotten some medals and didn't think this request was for anything important. After two weeks of prodding by the officers, he relented and agreed to the "trip." That flight ended up taking him to the White House to receive the Medal of Honor from President Lyndon Johnson.

When asked what the medal meant to him, Wetzel replied,

"When I was in the Tokyo hospital, where the doctors took out more than four hundred stitches, some of the guys I pulled out who were recovering from their wounds found out I was there. They would walk up to my bed and ask, 'Are you Gary Wetzel?' And I'd say, 'Yeah,' and they would pull out pictures of their wives, kids, or girlfriends and say, 'Hey, man, because of you, this is what I've got to go back to." Wetzel would reply, "I'm not Superman. I was just a guy doing his job."

To read this full story and the heart-stopping stories of over thirty more of our greatest war heroes, please check out our paperback Audiobook and eBook: *Giant Killers, War Heroes, and Special Forces Legends*. Available Now on Amazon, Amazon Audible, Apple, Spotify, Audiobooks.Com, Google Play, and most major platforms.

American Hero, Mercenary, Spy...

The incredible true story of the smallest man to ever serve in the U.S. military - Green Beret Captain Richard J. Flaherty

THE GIANT KILLER

David A. Yuzuk with Neil L. Yuzuk

INTRODUCTION

"Don't slide down the rabbit hole. The way down is a breeze but climbing back's a battle." —Kate Morton

"I have noticed that sometimes I frighten people; what they really fear is themselves. They think it is I who scare them, but it is the dwarf within them, the ape-faced manlike being who sticks up his head from the depths of their souls.

"Most dwarfs are buffoons. They have to make jokes and play trick to make their masters and guests laugh. I have never demeaned myself to anything like that. Nobody has even suggested that I should.

My very appearance forbids such a use of
me. My cast of countenance is unsuited
to ridiculous pranks. And I never laugh.
I am no buffoon. I am a dwarf and nothing but a dwarf."

—Par Lagerkvist

My name is David Yuzuk. As a veteran police officer I can affirm there are no words more chilling to hear than, "I have to tell you who I really am." This statement, uttered by a tiny homeless man, changed my life forever. It would be the last investigation in my twenty-year police career, dragging me down the rabbit hole of CIA conspiracies and stolen classified weapons. It would become a three-year journey of discovery stretching from the bloody jungles of Vietnam to the dangerous streets of Iraq and Venezuela, all in search of the peripatetic Captain Richard J. Flaherty. I would learn that not all of our teachers stand in front of a class or appear in the shape or image we envisioned they'd have. One of my teachers, seemingly forgotten by society, came to me later in life. The mantra he would incessantly preach was for me to discover my quest and live a life of no regret.

1

Dark Skies

Sometimes it's the journey that teaches you a lot about your destination."

— Drake

May 8, 2015

Aventura, Florida

As the afternoon's dark thunderstorm rolled in off the coast I backed my marked police car into an alleyway. The heavy raindrops hammered on my windshield as I searched through my papers for that phone number. It took me three days of digging — and a hell of a lot of favors — to get the number, and I didn't want to waste any more time, so I made the call.

A no-nonsense voice answered: "Hello."

"Hi. This is officer Yuzuk from the Aventura police department in Dade County, Florida. I'm trying to get ahold of retired ATF agent Fred Gleffe."

The voice warmed a bit. "Officer Yuzuk, I wasn't expecting your call so quickly. Look, I'm just finishing up some work in my garage. Is there something real fast I could help you with?"

"Yes sir. I wanted to check up on a man I've known for the last fifteen years who frequents my city. He mentioned that he worked undercover with you on a really big case."

"You got a name?" "Flaherty."

He paused long enough for me to check my phone to make sure the call wasn't dropped.

"Richard J. Flaherty. How is old Captain Flaherty these days?"

"Homeless," I reluctantly replied.

Gleffe paused, cleared his throat and replied, "Homeless ... that's a damn shame."

"Yes sir, it is."

"Richard was one hell of an undercover operator, and we certainly couldn't have gotten that case started without him."

I was shocked by the revelation and jerked up in my seat. "So, it's true?"

"Absolutely. Look, give me a call tomorrow and I'll go over the whole case with you."

"That would be great."

"Anything else?" Gleffe seemed more relaxed and expansive.

"Yeah, one last thing. Richard kind of figured I would check up on him. He asked me not to contact you, or anyone else involved in the case."

"Why is that?" Gleffe asked.

"He said if I asked too many questions it could be bad for my career — and dangerous to his health."

"Well, it's been over thirty years. I'm not sure about how much danger he would be in, although that operation did piss a lot of people off."

"He said it had to do with classified weapons," I added.

After another long pause, Gleffe finally said, "Let me think about the case and we'll talk more tomorrow. How about I give you a call from my office landline ... let's say around five p.m.?"

I noted a slight change in his voice. It seemed a little less friendly, but I kept the thought to myself and answered, "Yes sir, that sounds good. I really appreciate the help."

In south Florida as quickly as the afternoon summer thunderstorms roll in, they just as quickly dissipate. On the bustling business street a large and imposing shadow emerges from an alleyway.

The man casting the shadow is sixty-nine-year-old Richard James Flaherty. Although Richard would always claim that he was every bit of four-feet-nine inches tall, his actual medical records reveal he was only four-feet- seven-inches.

Close to seventy years old, he still walks with a sure step; his posture is ramrod straight despite the fact he is lugging a heavy backpack. Under his faded navy-blue T-shirt and blue jeans is the taut ninety-eight-pound muscular body he's maintained since his teens. Although small his body is perfectly proportioned, leading most who see him to think he is an athlete of some sort, perhaps a jockey or gymnast.

Flaherty walks into the local Publix supermarket, which has served as his base of operations for the last ten years. He quickly selects a ham and turkey sandwich and pays for it at the front cashier. Several customers stare at the tiny homeless man, some with curiosity and others with disgust. Flaherty avoids all eye contact and mutters to himself as he exits the business. It's the same chant he's been reciting over a lifetime filled with the frustration of how people react to him: *What the hell do they know about me?*

As Flaherty prepares to cross the street he quickly scans the bushes for the tell-tale signs of an enemy ambush. He could always sense an ambush by a tingling sensation he felt rolling down his arms and into his hands. Choosing a safe path before moving forward was as natural to him as breathing. His last priority was to keep his head on a swivel and check his six to make sure those State Department agents weren't close behind.

Is it time to move on? Time to find a new area to melt into? Am I still even on their radar? Of course I am ... I know too many of their damn secrets.

Although the State Department agents were always at the front of his mind, he wasn't all that sure about the helicopters he could glimpse flying off in the distance. He was positive they weren't standard police or news helicopters because the sound emitting from their main rotor blades was the distinctive, primal rhythmic thumping from a 1960s Bell UH-1 Iroquois Helicopter — better known as a Huey.

Flaherty heads toward the library, knowing that if the "government" ever needed his services again his point of contact would be a local public building where he could blend seamlessly into the crowd.

Flaherty walks inside the building, enjoying the feel of the refreshingly cool air conditioning as it surrounds his body. He inhales deeply, savoring the earthy almond smell the books give off commingled with a coffee aroma drifting from the staff's office.

He strolls over to a familiar aisle of books and hunts the crowded shelves for his target. Once located he stands on his toes and reaches as high up as he can to grasp *Paradise Lost*, by John Milton.

He takes the familiar book over to an empty corner desk and sits down with his back against the wall. He scans the room one more time until he feels it's safe, pulls out his sandwich and opens the book. Across the room, partially hidden in the shadows, a large man observes Flaherty.

As Flaherty is about to bite into his sandwich, his adversary bounds towards him and removes an "L"-shaped silver object from his front pants pocket.

Flaherty looks up from his book, but it's too late: his red-faced adversary is already standing over him, clutching an asthma inhaler. The inhaler emits a snake-like hiss into the obese library security guard's mouth as he depresses the trigger.

"This is the last time ... I'm going to warn you they don't want bums hanging out in here. Get your shit and get going."

Flaherty gathers his belongings without protest and exits the library. *Paradise Lost* is left open on the desk.

As the blazing sun starts to recede on the horizon another round of dark clouds rolls in from the ocean. Flaherty walks half a block towards his familiar shelter, a covered bus bench. He slides his heavy backpack off his shoulder and sits down on the metal bench next to a mother and her small daughter. Seeing Flaherty,

235

the mother protectively puts her arm around her child and draws her close.

An elderly grizzled homeless man walks by, extending his gnarled hand to beg the mother for change. She turns her back on the man and continues to shield her daughter from a world of threats.

Flaherty rips his sandwich in half and motions to the older man. The man swiftly snatches up the sandwich before the gift can be retracted. With a glance over his shoulder the man hurries off to a familiar isolated alcove in the bushes. Feeling as safe as he possibly can, this hunger-worn societal outcast devours his sandwich with huge wolfing bites.

Flaherty sits patiently at the bus bench as people stream on and off buses and crowds walk hurriedly up and down the street, passing him without notice.

All the while time stands still for Flaherty. He sits motionless and alone as the day turns to night. The brake lights from the herd of cars sitting in traffic reflect off of the shelter's plastic walls, painting Flaherty in an eerie red glow.

The storm clouds once again hang over the city, and with a rumbling belch the sky opens up with heavy sheets of rain. The deluge seals Flaherty inside his shelter, further isolating him from the world.

May 9, 2015 — 1:15 A.M. Aventura, Florida

Eight hours after my phone call to agent Gleffe the rain has stopped, and the streets are already bone dry. The parched earth has absorbed all the moisture it can, and Flaherty — after leaving his shelter — goes to sleep under his usual palm tree. He is sleeping in his customary upright position, with his backpack bolstered against the base of the tree for padding. Surrounding him are the dried crunchy leaves and twigs he nightly places around his perimeter to alert him if anyone comes near.

The faint sound of a helicopter startles him awake. Flaherty instinctually reaches for the memory of his Colt Python revolver holstered on his hip. As his eyes regain focus he scans the sky for the helicopter, only catching brief glimpses of a dark silhouette heading away from him. Flaherty stands up, grabs his backpack and heads off towards the empty city street. He stares into the cloudless dark sky, thankful for his most faithful midnight companion: the moon. *Finally, a break in the gloom.*

He cautiously crosses the street at the crosswalk and glances up several more times, looking for the helicopter. A pair of car headlights slice through the dark empty streets. As Flaherty is about to step onto the median a bright white light appears out of nowhere, catching him entirely by surprise.

A loud explosion of shattering glass and twisting metal mixes with the heavy thud of a one-hundred-pound man being struck by a car traveling at twenty-five miles per hour.

Flaherty is lifted over the front left bumper — his head crashes into the car's A-frame and side window. The violent impact causes the metal A-frame to warp, the side window to shatter. Flaherty is then violently propelled upward and forward, his backpack separating from his body to flip through the air. He crashes and tumbles in a violent landing fifteen feet away on the dirt of the median. Flaherty's backpack rolls forward onto the edge of the street as papers escape from its ripped sides.

As the car drives away the street light reflects off a tiny bloody sneaker finally coming to rest upright in the middle of the street.

––––––––––––––––––

The sun is rising over the beautiful Turnberry Isle golf course as an athletic male and female jogger round a corner of the walking path that runs adjacent to the golf course. Several lawn mowers drone in the background, and the smell of fresh-cut grass permeates the crisp morning air.

The early rising BMW-driving Starbucks crowd is just exiting their shiny high-rise condos, calculating which route to the office will cause the least amount of suffering in Miami's three-lane parking lots — ironically called 'highways'.

As the jogging couple crosses the street the woman notices a child's sneaker oddly lying in the middle of the road. As she gets closer to the sneaker she looks into the median, seeing a bloody pant leg and foot jutting out of the bushes. The rest of the person's body is obscured by foliage.

"Oh my God!" wails the horrified woman.

Flaherty Military Biography:

Special Forces Capt. Flaherty - In December of 1967, he was sent to Vietnam with the 101st Airborne Division. He served as a Platoon Leader with companies B, C, and D and a Recon Platoon Leader with Echo Company.

In January 1969, he returned to CONUS and attended the Special Forces School at Fort Bragg, where he was assigned to the 3rd Special Forces Group. Later that year, he returned to Southeast Asia with the 46th Special Forces Company A-110 in Camp Pawai, Lopburi, Thailand.

Captain Flaherty earned The Silver Star, 2 Bronze Stars W/Valor, 2 Purple Hearts, the Air Medal, a Gallantry Cross W/Silver Star, an Army Commendation Medal, a Combat Infantryman's Badge, 3 Overseas Bars, a Sharpshooter Badge W/Rifle Bar, a Air Medal, Parachutist Badge, Vietnam Service badge.

"It does not matter how slowly you go, so long as you do not stop."

—Confucius

About the Author

Born and raised in Brooklyn, N.Y., David attended the University of Stony Brook on a football scholarship. David moved to Miami and became a 19-year veteran of the Aventura Police Department, working as a uniformed road patrolman, undercover officer, and detective. David was awarded Officer of the Month on two separate occasions by his department and was recognized as Officer of the Month by the Dade County Chief's Association.

In 2017, he wrote and produced the critically acclaimed documentary, *The Giant Killer*, based on the epic life of his friend, Green Beret Captain Richard J. Flaherty. David's quest was to find the answers to his enigmatic friend's shadowy life and death.

The documentary was awarded The People's Choice Award at the Silicon Beach Film Festival, Best Film in the UK Monthly Film Festival, and was an official selection at the Rome International Film Festival and the Fort Lauderdale International Film Festival.

After five years of research, David completed and released the nonfiction book *The Giant Killer*. The book ran for years as an Amazon #1 Best Seller in Vietnam War Biographies. In March of 2023, David released his second military book, *Giant Killers, War Heroes, and Special Forces Legends*.

"Special thanks to Ginny Dornheggen and Laura Hines Kern for all the help making this book."

- David A. Yuzuk

Printed in Great Britain
by Amazon

60923723R00147